Trilateral Commission

Task Force Reports: 1-7

TRILATERAL COMMISSION

TASK FORCE REPORTS: 1-7

△ THE TRIANGLE PAPERS

A Compilation of Reports
from the First Two Years
of the Trilateral Commission

Published by
NEW YORK UNIVERSITY PRESS
New York: 1977

These reports were prepared for the Trilateral Commission and have been released under its auspices. Each report was discussed at a meeting of the Commission's Executive Committee — in Tokyo in October 1973, in Brussels in June 1974 or in Washington in December 1974. The Statements issued by the Executive Committee in Tokyo, Brussels and Washington were based in part upon them. The authors of the reports, who are experts from North America, Western Europe and Japan, have been free to present their own views. The Commission has made the reports available for wider distribution as a contribution to informed discussion and handling of the issues treated.

Copyright© 1977 by The Trilateral Commission
Library of Congress Catalog Card Number: 77-2476
ISBN: 0-8147-8159-4 (cloth)
0-8147-8160-8 (paper)

Manufactured in the United States of America

Table of Contents

Foreword

"Trilateralism" is now spelled with a small "t". The notion of a grouping consisting of Japan, North America and Western Europe has become more and more prominent in recent years. Undoubtedly, this reflects an economic and political reality — growing interpenetration and interdependence, among the major industrialized countries, and indeed on a global scale. Yet trilateralism has also been actively promoted, and the Trilateral Commission is one of the elements of recognition as well as promotion of the trilateral concept. That the Commission's work has not been altogether unsuccessful is indicated by the increasing demand for its reports, which led to this book — a compilation of the first seven task force reports to the Trilateral Commission.

Task force reports are one of the cornerstones of the work of the Commission. This volume presents the reports published during the first two years of Commission discussions. Each of the reports was prepared by three authors, one each from Japan, North America and Western Europe. In each case, the three authors consulted with a range of experts inside (and sometimes outside) the three regions.* Each paper has been discussed in draft form in a meeting of the Trilateral Commission, but the authors have been free to present their views and are jointly responsible for the published text. All the reports contain policy recommendations.

The element of debate is one of the most important and valuable aspects of the work of the Commission — intensive debate between the members of the Commission has helped to increase understanding between the three regions, and often, even to reach some form of consensus about the policy recommendations formulated by the three authors of a report.

The intensity of debate in the Trilateral Commission has been helped by the quality and heterogeneity of its members: Representatives of government and opposition parties, of labor and management and of the media and academia contribute their experience and knowledge

---

*The appendices of this volume list the consultants and meetings which comprised the "Trilateral Process" for each report.

in this private organization. They do not represent any particular organizations — which has helped to create the openness and constructiveness of discussions, and to establish a multidimensional link of communication between Japan, North America and Europe.

Differences of opinion continue, of course, within the organization, and are often reflected in the discussions. Yet at the same time it has often been possible to achieve a broad consensus among members on subjects such as those dealt with in these reports. This consensus was possible because of some convictions shared by all members — particularly the conviction that the cooperation of all three regions is essential to assure the smooth management of interdependence; cooperation based not on coercion and arm-twisting but on mutuality of interest, and indeed on the longer-term interests of mankind.

The trilateral countries bear a particular responsibility in this context. Their resources and power give them a special role in global politics. Their very weight obliges them to find constructive solutions taking into consideration not only their own interests, but also global concerns. Constructive policies in a world of rapid change, however, mean acceptance of change, mean reform, mean architecture constructively utilizing and combining the elements of change. Such policies mean more than muddling-through reactions to immediate crises — they involve the identification of problems on the horizon and beyond, and the formulation of concepts and long-term approaches to deal with them.

It is with this philosophy that the reports and recommendations reprinted in this volume should be read. Some of the suggestions contained in these reports have meanwhile become reality. The seventh report, from the task force on relations with developing countries, recommended that a "Third Window" be established by the World Bank which would annually provide $3 billion in additional concessional lending to developing countries in the 1976-1980 period. A scaled-down version of such a "Third Window" was put into operation in the Bank in 1975-76, and it appears the trilateral report played a role in gaining acceptance for this idea. The first report, prepared by the monetary task force in the fall of 1973, recommended the coordinated and joint sale of official gold holdings into private markets, with "capital gains" to be used for development assistance. To our knowledge, this was the first time such a proposal appeared in print. One of the authors, Richard N. Cooper (now U.S. Under Secretary of State for Economic Affairs), has written that the proposal was regarded as "quixotic" at the time, but it is being partially realized in the current IMF sale of a portion of its gold holdings, with the "capital gains" to be used for development assistance through a special trust fund.

That governments and international organizations have reacted positively to suggestions by the Trilateral Commission conveyed to them through our members is one indication of the value which our work has had so far. It is this fact which also has encouraged us to continue for another three-year period, up to mid-1979.*

GEORGES BERTHOIN, *European Chairman*

GERARD C. SMITH, *North American Chairman*

TAKESHI WATANABE, *Japanese Chairman*

March 1977

---

*More information about the Commission and its activities can be obtained from the regional secretariats in Paris (151 boulevard Haussmann), Tokyo (c/o Japan Center for International Exchange, 4-9-17 Minami-Azabu, Minato-ku), and New York (345 East 46th Street).

TOWARDS A RENOVATED

WORLD MONETARY SYSTEM

Motoo Kaji
PROFESSOR
Tokyo University

Richard N. Cooper
PROVOST
Yale University

Claudio Segré
BANKER
Paris

Table of Contents

2

I.

INTRODUCTION: DEFINITION OF THE PROBLEM AND THE PRESENT STATE OF DISCUSSIONS

Two problems reside at the core of the world economy of modern, mixed-economy industrial nations. The first problem is how to achieve full employment without drifting into rapid inflation, which arises from attempts to pursue conflicting and contradictory objectives without adequate instruments of policy. Monetary management gave governments a great weapon to deal with the periodic depressions that plagued pre-World War II economies; but this same management of money set economies adrift in terms of the real value of their monetary units. Attempts to maintain full employment may, under the ever present pressure for greater real wages, lead to severe inflation.

The second problem is how to combine managed national economies, with their national pursuit of national objectives, into an open, harmonious, and mutually beneficial world economy. Governmental attempts to influence domestic economic events may be frustrated by the movement of funds and firms across national frontiers, and they will be tempted to take defensive action, possibly damaging to other countries.

The first problem is one that all industrial countries face in common, but the solution must mainly come from within; the second is a joint problem that all industrial countries must face together in search of cooperative agreement.

The International Monetary System—the formal rules, the informal conventions, and the institutional arrangements for dealing with financial relations among nations — represents an important, perhaps the most important, component of a harmonious international economic system.

The International Monetary System worked remarkably well until the late 1960's. The growth of production and international trade has been unprecedented. The Bretton Woods Agreement of 1944 laid down the basic rules and established the International Monetary Fund (IMF) to oversee their application. The U.S. dollar emerged after World War II as an international currency that provided liquidity, elasticity, and financial stability to the international monetary system. But confidence in the dollar — and in the system itself — depended *inter alia* on a well man-

3

aged American economy, and that precondition ceased to be met in the late 1960's. Moreover, the growing use of a national currency as an international one ultimately contained the seeds of its own destruction, for sooner or later its convertibility into gold would inevitably have become impaired. It was partly a matter of luck that dollar outflows served world liquidity needs so well for so many years. In addition, financial assets achieved an international mobility to a degree that was totally unanticipated at Bretton Woods, a mobility with which indeed the resulting Agreement was not suited to cope.

The task before us is to renovate the monetary system so that it can do as well in the next two decades as it did in the two decades following the second World War, recognizing that the underlying conditions at present are very different from what they were in the 1940's.

This post-war monetary system formally broke down in August 1971, when the United States declared that the U.S. dollar was no longer convertible into gold or indeed into any other reserve asset, although the system had shown severe strain even before then. The Smithsonian Agreement of December 1971 brought some relief, but the relief could only be temporary because that agreement represented a stopgap rather than a basic reform of the monetary system and because several major participants, notably Britain and the United States, did not fully accept the exchange rates that were then agreed. Britain broke away from the Smithsonian pattern of exchange rates in June 1972 by floating its currency, and the United States broke with the pattern by devaluing the dollar in February 1973. Massive movements of funds across foreign exchanges and uncertainty about the future of the monetary system led to a general pattern of floating exchange rates in March 1973, followed by a surprising and fundamentally unwarranted depreciation of the dollar, combined with erratic day-to-day movements of the dollar rate and widespread uncertainty about currency values.

In September 1972 the Committee of Twenty finance ministers was established to provide a negotiated basis for improvements in the international monetary system. Their deliberations have proceeded with care, and their results will necessarily be long in coming, for disagreement remains deep on several issues central to a coherent system. They agreed on an outline for further work at Nairobi in September 1973.

A renovated international monetary system cannot offer a panacea for all economic ills. In particular, its contribution to solving the problem of world inflation, which is fundamentally domestic in origin, is positive

4

but not decisive. The monetary system can influence the extent to which inflationary or contractionary impulses are transmitted from one nation to another; and it can also determine the degree of success in achieving a mutually beneficial division of labor among nations, raising living standards for all.

We do not at present have a coherent international monetary "system;" and we court the risk of losing the substantial gains of the past three decades through a progressive deliberalization of international transactions. There is an urgent need to restore some systematic, mutually agreed international monetary order. A renovated system must command acceptance by all major participants, and it must contain a certain degree of resilience against major economic disturbances of all kinds, including mistakes in economic policy, which are bound to occur from time to time under the political pressures and counterpressures of democratic regimes and the struggles to achieve or maintain power in nondemocratic ones. A renovated system must also address the question of what international currency is to prevail in the world, since one or another is bound to emerge, and what will be the conventions governing capital movements, including the proper role for the eurocurrency markets.

Agreement among the leading industrial countries is a necessary condition for a smoothly functioning international monetary system. Their concerns and interests must be accommodated. But this does not mean that they alone have an interest in a smoothly functioning international monetary system. On the contrary, perhaps the greatest proportionate beneficiaries will be the developing countries, whose dependence on international trade and capital for rising standards of living is even greater than that of the large industrial countries, and who therefore have a substantial stake in successful resolution of the present difficulties. Harmony among the leading industrial countries is of the utmost importance to the economic welfare of the developing nations.

As a practical matter, the Communist countries of the world have lain outside the "world" monetary system of the past three decades. For the intermediate future, they will continue to lie outside the system, for the differences in their methods of price determination and their modes of economic exchange from those of mixed economies remain sufficiently great that interaction between the two regions, while growing, will continue to be small relative to economic interactions within the non-Communist portions of the world. Greater exchange with Communist countries should be sought wherever it is possible and mutually advantageous.

Growing world demand for energy, combined with the high natural concentration of petroleum reserves, especially in the Middle East, means that large earnings will accrue over the next decade to countries with relatively small population. This concentration of mobile wealth in the hands of a relatively few countries, not as yet well integrated into the community of nations, creates a possible source of disturbance to financial markets, to foreign exchange markets, and to the orderly functioning of the international monetary system.

We have not attempted to address the problems of or posed by these three important groups of countries — the poor countries, the Communist countries, and the oil producing countries. The issues involved go far beyond the operation of the international monetary system, and since the monetary aspects cannot be discussed satisfactorily without addressing other basic issues, these problems are best left to further work by other task forces of the Trilateral Commission. We believe that the proposals we make below for improvements in the international monetary system are fully compatible with a satisfactory evolution of relations with these countries, and indeed may contribute constructively to that end. In what follows, however, we address the International Monetary System principally from the viewpoint of the non-Communist industrial countries.

II.

Differences in National Policies and Perspectives

All of our countries wish to see the restoration of orderly economic relationships among themselves. However, at present there exist considerable divergences in national policies and perspectives. These divergences stem partly from the fact that each country puts priority on domestic objectives, a priority that is to some extent unavoidable, and that among domestic objectives relative priorities differ from country to country. They stem partly also from substantial differences in economic and political structure, with the relative dependence on foreign trade, the degree of industrialization, and the mode of political decision-making varying markedly from country to country. The divergences have been aggravated in recent years by deterioration in mutual confidence. We do not consider the differences in structure or in priorities sufficiently great to make impossible a restoration of world economic order. But a renovated system cannot be realized without first restoring mutual confidence and, with that, a degree of tolerance for diversity of view and circumstance. Better understanding will reduce the present gaps in perspective.

Differences of view often take technical form, but they are not merely technical. Rather, they reflect differences in conception, in condition, and in conventions, conventions that are often based on historical circumstances no longer applicable. These three kinds of differences are often comingled on the same issue. Fortunately, purely national perspectives are rare. It is a sign of maturity in the modern era that differences of view are at least as wide within nations as between them. We identify some of the differences to illustrate their depth and their fundamentally political nature, insofar as basic conceptions must be considered political. By the same standard, our later recommendations also reflect political judgment.

Fundamental differences of view concern the extent to which the international monetary system should — or can — impose "discipline" on domestic economic policies. Some observers believe that the international system should provide a major bastion against excessive economic expansion. Others believe that it should not. Still others believe that it *cannot* provide such a bastion in modern democracies that have all experienced and used the benefits of managed money. These divergent views are found within most countries.

A second fundamental difference of view, also found within most countries, but to significantly varying degrees, concerns the freedom that should be accorded to international capital movements. Some observers view international capital movements as a major vehicle for economic progress. Others view them as a major source of economic disturbance and therefore a deterrent to economic progress. Still others view capital movements more neutrally, but fear that capital movements cannot be controlled effectively even when on normative grounds a case can be made that they should be. Yet others entertain a sharp distinction on these various grounds between short- and long-term capital movements.

Resentment has been voiced about the "special privilege" of the United States residing in the international use of the dollar; concern has been especially focussed on United States direct investment abroad financed, not by a surplus of goods and services, but by IOU's on the United States picked up by foreign central banks. The United States, for its part, has emphasized the economic costs of the dollar's role and the special responsibilities it carries in the areas of mutual security, and it has badgered other nations to contribute more. Behind much of this debate, brought openly to the surface by the late President de Gaulle, is anxiety over national status in the community of nations, and the special status that having a reserve currency seems to confer.

Yet another area in which difference of opinion is sharp concerns the degree to which exchange rates should be relied upon as a principal mechanism of adjustment in the international monetary system. While all parties recognize the need for some exchange rate adjustment, some feel that this adjustment should be resisted as much as possible, partly on grounds that exchange rate changes do their work only slowly and imperfectly, partly on grounds that extensive reliance on changes in exchange rates will be disintegrative rather than integrative in their influence on the world economy. Others feel that the evolution of national economies has been such as to require much greater flexibility of exchange rates than was enjoyed until the summer of 1971. They argue that the alternative to exchange rates, in general much heavier reliance on controls of international transactions, is likely to be far more disintegrative in its influence than is greater flexibility of exchange rates.

It is increasingly recognized that the arguments on exchange rates do not apply with equal force to all countries, and that relative fixity of rates may be highly desirable within certain groups of countries. More-over, the European Community has embarked on the difficult task of achieving monetary integration by the end of the decade and has chosen the course of attempting to reduce exchange rate fluctuations among member countries. It thus finds itself pulled in two directions at the present time, toward somewhat greater flexibility in its relations with the rest of the world and toward less flexibility within Europe. The internal objective inevitably influences its approaches to the broader system.

There are also divergences of view on seemingly technical issues — whether and when and under what circumstances the dollar can become convertible into other reserve assets; whether surplus countries should carry precisely the same responsibilities for balance of payments adjust-ment as do countries in deficit; whether it is vital to maintain existing export industries at all cost, despite continuing large payments surplus; and whether gold should continue to play an integral role in the mone-tary system. Divergence on the last issue seems now to be much dimin-ished as a result of the wildly erratic movements of gold prices on private markets in the summer of 1973, and now that gold is no longer neces-sary as a surrogate for raising questions about the special status of the dollar.

Irritation has especially been expressed over the seemingly "benign neglect" attitude of the U.S. government toward economic developments abroad and toward the evolution of the monetary system, and its ap-parent disdain of advance consultation in matters, such as import sur-charges and export controls, that vitally affect the interests and welfare of its leading trading partners. Differences have also persisted on the interpretation of unfolding events, and especially of the U.S. balance of payments deficit, undeniably too large for too many years. Declining competitiveness, excessive capital outflows, large burdens of aid and de-fense, foreign need for dollars and foreign unwillingness to adjust, and many other explanations have been invoked to explain the large deficit, too often in a search for blame and a spirit of recrimination.

We believe that some of these many differences of view will dis-appear with continuing frank discussion and consultation. But we also believe that some differences will remain, even after the compromises that inevitably must be made in an attempt at reconciliation in achieving common ground for renovating the international monetary system. An important feature of a renovated system is precisely its scope for accommodation of nations with widely different circumstances and even with somewhat different basic preferences regarding the objectives of economic policy. It must be resilient both to differences in condition and to errors in policy. The section that follows attempts to lay down the principal features of a renovated system.

III.

BASIC ELEMENTS OF A RENOVATED SYSTEM

Despite divergent perspectives and in some cases fundamental disagreement on detail, there is now wide convergence of view on the areas that require improvement in the international monetary system. In this section, we discuss those areas and offer our view, in general terms, on the appropriate dimensions of renovation:

1. balance of payments adjustment;
2. reserve assets and convertibility;
3. the problem of outstanding balances;
4. growing economic interdependence, calling for greater harmony in national economic policies; and
5. institutional aspects of this renovated monetary system.

1. BALANCE OF PAYMENTS ADJUSTMENT

Many economic forces, continually changing, affect each nation's balance of international payments. One of the most common influences arises when a country's economy enters a period of excessive or deficient expansion of demand in relation to the country's domestic economic objectives. Excessive expansion of demand will typically worsen the balance of payments, although in the present era of high capital mobility occasions may arise in which the tight money associated with excessive expansion improves the balance of payments, as it did for the United States in 1969. Deficient expansion in domestic demand, on the other hand, will typically improve the balance of payments. Under either circumstance, actions to direct the domestic economy back onto the preferred course will help to correct the balance of payments, and no special action therefore needs to be taken to correct the disequilibrium in the balance of payments.

There are, however, also many other forces — stemming from technological change, from international differences in growth in incomes and output, from discoveries and exhaustion of natural resources, from changes in taste, and from many other factors — that influence the balance of payments and that may create imbalance in payments. An effective international monetary system must have some method for eliminating payments imbalances as they arise under the pressure of these various influences.

The Bretton Woods System, which was formally in force from the late 1940's until 1971, relied in the main on a combination of short-term financing and exchange rate adjustment. As that system worked in practice, exchange rate adjustment was often too late, too one-sided toward currency depreciation, and when it came, too large. The system relied to a greater extent than had been planned on trade quotas and on inflation or deflation in domestic demand. It took for granted controls on capital movements. By the time a "fundamental disequilibrium" gave rise to a change in an exchange rate, the need for such change was apparent to many observers and that in turn gave rise to large and disruptive flows of speculative funds. The large exchange rate adjustments for their part administered substantial shocks to economies, since calculations of profit and loss had been made with quite different expectations. These deficiencies suggest that future exchange rate changes should be smaller and if necessary more frequent as corrective measures. *We believe that a renovated monetary system should impose substantial pressure for timely exchange rate changes, by countries in surplus as well as by countries in deficit.* Changes in exchange rates, however, will not produce the expected results unless they are accompanied by domestic monetary and fiscal actions appropriate for making the change effective.

The time may come when the need for exchange rate changes diminishes as national economies become ever more closely linked to one another and as this evolution leads to a harmonization of national economic objectives and of national economic policies. But that day is still far off for the world as a whole. In the meantime, changes in exchange rates will be necessary for keeping national economies in line in a liberal world economic setting.

One of the most difficult tasks in balance of payments adjustment is identifying those cases in which domestic action in pursuit of generally agreed domestic economic objectives will alone be sufficient to deal with imbalances in payments, and separating them from those cases in which direct action on the exchange rate is required to correct an imbalance of payments. Broadly speaking, the pre-1971 system erred too heavily in avoiding changes in exchange rates when they were in fact desirable. The renovated monetary system should correct that; there should be a much heavier presumption in favor of altering exchange rates, recognizing that in so shifting the presumption, some errors of the opposite type will be created.

In sorting out cases in which exchange rates should not be made from those in which they should be, the economic developments of major countries should be kept under continuous review by the revamped International Monetary Fund, along the lines discussed below, so that cumulatively large disequilibria are not permitted to develop. If changes in exchange rates seem to be indicated, refusal by a country to introduce such changes should invoke sanctions by the international community. For a country in balance of payments deficit these sanctions might involve refusal to lend to it for financing its payments deficit. For a country in balance of payments surplus, the sanction might involve financial measures such as non-payment of interest on reserves above a certain level; and *in extremis* might involve imposition of import surcharges, under international surveillance, against its goods — that is, a de facto partial revaluation of its currency through the trade policies of other countries. If these possible sanctions are effective in their intent, they will of course never have to be used, for they will encourage the appropriate adjustment actions well before the sanctions would be brought into play.

It has been suggested that exchange rates should be allowed to float freely, determined solely by the market forces of supply and demand. Reform along these lines is neither practicable nor desirable. For most countries the exchange rate remains one of the most important single economic variables. As long as governments are held responsible for national economic development, they cannot abdicate all responsibility for movements in the exchange rate. Freely floating exchange rates run the risk that occasional speculative forces may push the exchange rate far from a position that is warranted on fundamental economic grounds. Appropriate government policy calls ultimately for management of the exchange rate, just as appropriate government policy these days calls for management of domestic monetary conditions.

A par value system, if properly managed, can provide adequate exchange rate flexibility. A "par value" system is one in which each country declares a fixed relationship between its currency and the primary reserve asset in any proposed system. Market rates may vary on either side of the par value within a permissible band of flexibility. A system of managed exchange rates without par values could, without undue complication, also provide a satisfactory combination of flexibility and stability. Rules for exchange market intervention would be required to ensure the consistent and harmonious evolution of exchange rates. We have not adopted this approach here, however, so we do not develop in detail what a system of that type might look like.

2. RESERVE ASSETS AND CONVERTIBILITY

During the 1950's and the early 1960's the international monetary system came to rely heavily on the United States dollar as a functioning reserve asset. This dependency had certain advantages, especially in the elastic provision of liquidity, but it also had disadvantages that have now become clear. Reliance on the dollar (or indeed on any national currency) places the reserve currency country in a special position that can be abused and is likely to generate resentment in other countries. Excessive outflows of dollars in the late 1960's and early 1970's led to the suspension of convertibility of the dollar into gold and Special Drawing Rights, which in turn led to the general floating which came into effect in March 1973. A renovated system needs to place the new Special Drawing Rights (SDRs) in a position of primacy among reserve assets. SDRs, properly managed, can provide for adequate and controlled growth in world liquidity. Under the system of exchange rate parities that we envisage, all currencies including the dollar would be convertible to SDRs at a fixed but alterable price. The United States would be expected to finance any payments deficits by drawing on its holdings of Special Drawing Rights.

If ever greater reliance is to be placed upon SDRs, the nature of the SDR must be improved. To that end, *we would* (i) *abolish the holding limits and the reconstitution provision of the present SDR;* (ii) *raise interest rates closer to interest rates on alternative reserve assets, but with allowance for the special character of the SDR;* and (iii) *break the formal tie to gold.* We would also give the SDR a distinctive designation, not dependent on acronyms constructed on the basis of national languages, to underline its monetary independence. We can think of no more fitting term than *"bancor,"* the designation J. M. Keynes used in his proposal for the creation of a postwar international financial institution, later to become the International Monetary Fund. We would however, retain for some time the requirement that bancor be used only for financing balance of payments deficits, thus discouraging its use for the conscious shifting of reserve assets from one form to another.

We envisage that bancor would be an abstract unit of account. From a formal point of view, it would be fully defined at any moment in time by its relationship through par values to all currencies of the world. In day-to-day operation, it would be defined by market exchange rates through some designated currency. We feel that this approach is far simpler than the "bouquet of currencies" approach to the definition of bancor that has sometimes been discussed.

We also envisage that bancor would become a unit of account in many private international transactions, and that financial instruments might be denominated in bancor. Monetary authorities should not impede this development. Eventually bancor might circulate as a genuine international currency and be used as a medium for an intervention in exchange markets, but that development would take place only gradually and is beyond the period with which we are concerned. It would of course require widening the eligibility for holding SDRs, from central banks alone, to include other financial institutions and even individuals.

The stipulation that bancor is to meet all global liquidity needs implies that *the United States and all other countries must finance their balance of payments deficits only by using reserve assets, not through the foreign acquisition of additional dollars or other reserve currencies.* This is the convertibility requirement. Conversion would be obligatory for the United States even when other countries chose to add to their dollar holdings, which they would remain free to do. Thus international control would be assured over global liquidity creation, but individual countries would be left free to choose the particular assets they desire to hold in their reserves, insofar as those assets arose from current balance of payments surpluses. They could not, however, convert at will dollars acquired in one period directly into bancor at a later period.

The need to finance deficits with bancor or other reserve assets, by each country standing ready to convert foreign official acquisitions of its currency into other reserve assets at a known price, implies the need to defend that price from time to time. This could become a constraining factor on domestic economic policy. The key judgment that must be made in the renovated monetary system is when to defend the fixed price between each national currency and bancor and when to alter it. This issue is, in a different form, the same issue as that discussed above in connection with how often to require changes in exchange rates for balance of payments adjustment. There will inevitably be occasional disagreements over just how far a country should be expected to go in adjusting its domestic economic policies so as to defend a fixed exchange rate before a change in that exchange rate becomes generally acceptable. What is needed is a framework in which such disagreements can be discussed and resolved. *That framework should involve both general presumptive guidelines for balance of payments adjustment, requiring for example that substantial reserve movements in either direction should lead to balance of payments adjustment actions, and a procedure for evaluation of alleged special circumstances and for resolution of disagreements.* Individual nations would formally be free to determine their exchange rates, so their nominal sovereignty would be unimpaired. But they would have this freedom only with accountability to the community of nations, and by violating the collective judgment of other nations they would run the risk of incurring the sanctions discussed above.

It has frequently been proposed that a link be established between the creation of international liquidity and the provision of development assistance by allocating a substantial share of newly created SDRs directly or indirectly to developing countries. This proposal represents a major issue in current discussions of reform of the monetary system, and it addresses a major problem of the world community. We accept the importance of the problem, but we do not favor this particular solution to it. Creation of international money involves a new, bold, and still fragile experiment. Until it is fully established, the SDR, revamped or not into bancor, will be under some suspicion. It is necessary to build confidence in such a new asset, resting on the cooperation of many countries, and confidence can come only gradually through experience with its successful creation and use. Establishment of a link to development assistance runs a serious risk of undermining confidence in the new asset before it is fully established. Moreover, it is doubtful that separation between the creation of bancor to serve the needs of international liquidity and its use for development assistance could be successfully sustained. Occasions will surely arise when the claims for control of world liquidity and the always pressing claims of developing countries for the transfer of additional resources will conflict. There is no assurance that the former claims will dominate, as they must if international liquidity is to be successfully controlled. The doubts of skeptics about managed international money will be reinforced under these conditions. Finally the creation of international money does not in itself generate the real resources which are required to be transferred to less developed countries. We believe it is preferable to take direct measures, through national fiscal action, to generate those resources.

Relations between the developed and the less developed countries will be the subject of analysis by another group, and we cannot do justice to this complex topic here. We simply state our strong support for substantially greater transfer of resources to less developed countries than is now taking place. We suggest one mechanism below for helping to accomplish this objective. There are many others as well that do not court the risk of undermining the new international reserve asset before it is fully established.

3. OUTSTANDING BALANCES

The presence of large outstanding official balances, a legacy of past United States balance of payments deficits, threatens any system of convertibility and may lead to unwarranted and unacceptable changes in exchange rates. These balances represent a heavy psychological burden, which in the spring of 1973 depressed the market for the dollar. A renovated international system requires some mechanism for dealing with this "overhang" of dollar balances. *We favor a system whereby countries that hold dollar balances can convert them into bancor in a new International Monetary Fund account, called a substitution account.* This would be done in a single, special issue of bancor. In this way countries with excessive dollars can get what effectively amounts to an exchange rate guarantee. The interest rate on bancor would obviously influence the extent of conversion, and it is partly to encourage such conversion that we suggest the interest rate be raised well above the present 1½ percent on SDRs.

The International Monetary Fund in turn would work out a mutually satisfactory arrangement with the United States to cover the exchange risk on the dollars that it acquired and to provide for their amortization over a suitably long period of time. Those countries that desire to hold dollars could continue to do so, but they would be under no pressure to hold dollars; thus it could be assumed that after consolidation all dollars remaining outstanding were willingly held.

This arrangement alone, while removing a major burden overhanging exchange markets, would not be able to deal with the problem of large conversions of private or remaining official dollar balances into other currencies in a short period of time. Under the renovated system, the United States would be obliged to convert any such dollars into reserve assets on demand; but it might not have reserve assets adequate to this task. One possibility would be to allow the dollar, or any currency under similar pressure, to float freely downward under such circumstances. But, by general agreement, such depreciation might not always be desirable. *It is therefore necessary to provide for large and rapid short-term lending to countries suddenly confronted with a conversion requirement which they cannot meet out of reserves and which it would be unadvisable to meet through exchange rate adjustment.* While this lending facility could be simply an enlargement of the present central bank swap facilities, we prefer a more formal institutional arrangement which in effect multilateralizes the swaps and lodges them within the International Monetary Fund, making it a true lender of last resort, a central bank for central banks.

This new facility would lend quickly and on short term any amount that a country seemed to require to defend an exchange rate that was threatened by a massive movement of funds. If, as would usually be the case, the movement of funds proved to be temporary, the borrowing country would repay the IMF as the reversals occurred. These loans might bear a high interest rate for the purpose of encouraging prompt repayment as well.

This type of emergency lending would not in principle be available to finance basic balance of payments deficits. But of course at the time of a massive movement of funds it is not generally possible to distinguish one type of funds from another. Where it is clear that the movement of funds is due to a basic balance of payments deficit the lending authorities could decline to lend. But generally the lending should be available to cover any type of massive switch from one currency to another, including a switch made by the residents of the country experiencing the run. If after a large flow it was learned that a portion of it was due to a worsening of the country's balance of payments position, then the country would be obliged to repay the IMF for any unwarranted borrowing, if necessary by drawing on the normal lending facilities of the IMF based on quotas, which would continue to function as now, and to take corrective steps.

If, on the other hand, the switch of funds or some part of it proved to be a lasting phenomenon, and not arising from a basic payments deficit, the short-term obligation that the borrowing country had incurred to the lending facility could be converted into a long-term interest-bearing debt with a fixed amortization schedule over a suitably long period of time. This in effect would represent a delayed consolidation operation of the type described above. The interest and amortization payments would be normal international payments and would, other things being equal, trigger the reformed adjustment process to allow the country to run the required surplus in its other international payments to repay the debt. The maturity would be sufficiently long, 40 years for example, so that the debt amortization would not unduly strain the adjustment process.

Such a facility would have special relevance to the United States because of the very large amount of dollars held abroad in private hands. But Britain would also benefit, for private sterling balances remain large, and increasing amounts of such other currencies as German marks, Swiss francs, and Japanese yen are being held by non-residents. So the problem is becoming a more general one and this new facility would offer a general solution. Moreover, we should not forget the even larger private resident balances in every currency. While movements abroad of resident funds are more readily subject to capital controls than is true for non-resident funds, large movement of such resident funds will nonetheless be possible in practice, as both France and Italy have learned in recent years, despite controls. Unless national reserves are to be large enough to cope with this contingency in the face of growing knowledge by the public everywhere of foreign exchange transactions, the lender-of-last-resort function would also cover such movements, which, of course, would be largely reversible.

4. ECONOMIC INTERDEPENDENCE

Even with improvements along the lines suggested above, the major industrial countries would be left with the problem of growing economic interdependence, which links national economies together ever more tightly. A beneficial division of labor is permitted by this growing interdependence, but it also leads to new constraints on national economic policy. The effectiveness of much national economic policy depends to a considerable degree on the insulation of the national economy from the world economy. As mobility of goods, funds, and factors of production increases, this insulation becomes thinner and thinner, and divergences in national economic policies lead to private responses that at once may create disturbances to other countries and erode the effectiveness of the policies of the country in question.

The most obvious and acute area where these developments have occurred is monetary policy. With increasingly mobile private funds, a country pursuing easy monetary policy finds itself simply encouraging a capital outflow, while a country trying to tighten up domestic monetary conditions simply encourages a capital inflow. Yet these very flows undercut the domestic purposes of monetary policy. Inflows of funds from abroad erode a government's capacity to tighten monetary conditions and damp down domestic demand, for example. In addition, the independent pursuit of national monetary policy may cause severe disturbances in other countries. An attempt by one country to tighten up its monetary conditions may lead to a competitive rise in interest rates. The dominance of large countries in this regard is especially felt and resented.

At the same time, so long as national economies are not fully integrated, nations will need to preserve some autonomy in national policy. Exchange rate flexibility within a band around parities will provide some of this necessary insulation between national economies, but not enough. Controls on capital movements represent an alternative, and they indeed can also provide some insulation between national economies. But as mobility increases further, any given set of controls becomes less and less workable. To provide insulation the controls must be extended to ever greater numbers of transactions, and the process of this extension will cut down the manifold advantages of an economic environment relatively free of controls. *We believe the appropriate course of action is for all industrial countries to shift the emphasis in domestic stabilization policy from monetary to fiscal measures,* where the impact on domestic economic activity continues to be high. In particular, *governments that do not have it need to be given the authority to move quickly and in the required degree to ease or tighten fiscal conditions,* and all governments need also to be charged with the responsibility for using fiscal policy flexibility.

In this way, divergences in national monetary policy need not be nearly so great as they have been in the past, and over the course of time the industrial nations can evolve a *common* monetary policy for the world community as a whole. We recognize, however, that the evolution toward flexible fiscal policy and a common monetary policy will be slow, for existing practices and constraints vary markedly from country to country.

5. THE INSTITUTIONAL SETTING

Many of the arrangements discussed above could be agreed and implemented among the major industrial countries alone. Because of their size and economic importance, their cooperation on these issues is essential. But other countries also have a vital interest in the evolution of the world economy, and as time passes a number of countries that are now economically "small" will grow in relative importance. For these reasons, *we believe a serious attempt should be made to lodge responsibility for overseeing and in some cases managing the improvements sketched above in an international institution, most logically a revamped International Monetary Fund.* But the Fund must be given more authority than it now has in guiding balance of payments adjustment, it must be capable of responding to financial need more quickly and in much larger magnitude than it is now able to do, and it must involve more actively the top policy-makers of the leading countries.

To accomplish this, we propose that the "Deputies" of the Ministerial Committee of Twenty, made up of top sub-cabinet monetary officials from national governments, be given a permanent place in the structure of the International Monetary Fund. They would meet as often as needed, at least six times a year, for the purpose of overseeing the renovated adjustment process and evaluating the use of the lender-of-last-resort facility, with assistance from the International Monetary Fund staff. Large countries have particular responsibility for assuring a smooth operation of the international monetary system. The relative importance of countries in the Fund should not be frozen, however; it should reflect and respond to changes in their relative importance in the world economy.

Present operations of the International Monetary Fund, including periodic review of national economic conditions, conditional lending for balance of payments support, and responsibility for evaluating the secular growth of world liquidity and proposing additions to it, would continue.

IV.

RISKS INHERENT IN THE PRESENT SITUATION

What are the consequences of failing to renovate the international monetary system quickly enough along the lines indicated above? We have attempted to suggest in general terms what a reformed system would look like. We have not provided a fully worked-out plan, however. A number of the suggested measures have functional equivalents, so a renovated system need not take the precise form we have outlined. But we have identified the basic issues that must be dealt with. This section concerns the risks of not dealing with them all. What are the dangers arising from simply allowing major currencies to "float" against one another as they have done in the period following March 1973, confirming the complete breakdown of the Bretton Woods system?

We have identified above the weaknesses of the Bretton Woods payments system as it evolved in practice. We are well aware of the weaknesses of a system in which exchange rates are too rigidly fixed. However, at the present time, we are in a period in which exchange rates are generally "floating" with ad hoc and uncoordinated intervention by central banks, each on its own volition. That system also has its weaknesses and dangers. We do not believe that the renovated system we propose can come into being quickly. We therefore must address the consequences of simply carrying on with present arrangements. The risks will, of course, vary substantially from country to country, in view of their different circumstances. Some countries will find the present arrangements far more tolerable, and even favorable, than others. But we do not believe that the present arrangements are durable, and we offer our reasons here. Some observers will view them as exaggerated, but we are citing risks, not certainties; and we believe the risks to be real, even if not certain to come about.

The first risk, as we learned in mid-1973, is that "floating" exchange rates will be subject to many pressures that are irrelevant to the preservation of equilibrium in a country's international payments, but will nevertheless cause disturbance to normal trade flows and through them to domestic economies, dependent on international trade as all our economies are today. Sharp movements in exchange rates unwarranted by fundamental economic considerations can occur in any currency, but they are especially likely where, as in the case of the dollar, sterling, the

German mark, and the Swiss franc, outstanding holdings of the currency are large relative to week-to-week international transactions in these currencies. (Of course, once allowance is made for large resident holdings of national currencies, this problem potentially becomes a general one. But conditions must usually deteriorate enormously before there is a wholesale speculation by residents against their own currency.) In these cases large movements in an exchange rate may take place in response to relatively small shifts in or out of the currency, and such shifts may well be governed by psychological or political factors affecting "confidence" in the currency and by subjective assessments of what other holders will do next rather than by fundamental economic factors that determine the strength of a currency over a longer period of time. Yet sharp shifts in exchange rates can have important ramifications for those whose livelihood depends on trade or on financial transactions with foreigners.

Modern governments, responsible for national economic developments, cannot allow arbitrary disturbances to impinge on domestic business activity through the exchange rate. They are likely to take steps to protect the domestic economy from these disturbances. They may do this by intervening in the foreign exchange market to restrict movements of the exchange rate. But an exchange rate is intrinsically two-sided and two countries may take very different views on what their common exchange rate should be. If so, they will intervene in the exchange market at cross purposes, and neither will wholly succeed. In the absence of some form of cooperation, countries will turn to other measures to provide the necessary protection. They may also turn to other measures to avoid having to take an exchange risk on foreign exchange reserves that would have to be acquired and held in connection with exchange market intervention. A country that desires to avoid appreciation of its currency would impose controls on the importation of capital and possibly on the export of goods. A country that wants to neutralize the trade and employment effects of what it regards as an under-valued currency would impose controls on imports from the country with the under-valued currency. These actions would be taken to protect the viability of domestic firms against what is perceived as predatory increases in foreign competitiveness transmitted through the exchange market. By assumption, these actions would take place in a context where coordination with other countries would be minimal. There would be no procedure for resolving conflicts in national objectives or inconsistencies in the national use of instruments of policy. The whole point of an agreed set of rules is to assure the *mutual* benefits that accrue in an orderly system as compared with a disorderly one.

A proliferation of controls on trade and capital movements would damage not only the direct participants, but third parties as well. In particular, developing countries would suffer great damage in an environment in which major industrial countries are competing with one another to erect barriers to trade and capital movements, just as they bore the brunt of a number of measures, such as tied aid, that were taken to protect over-valued currencies when exchange rates were too rigid. We do *not* see the danger of a major depression. Modern governments are too sensitive to unemployment to allow that to happen. What we do fear is a widespread use of controls on international transactions precisely to assure the autonomy governments may feel necessary to preserve national employment.

While we do not see a world depression, we do believe that such an evolution could result in major economic dislocations and in reduced standards of living. There would be temporary unemployment in those activities most heavily dependent on foreign trade. The standard of economic well-being would decline for all, relative to what it would otherwise be, but it would decline especially for those countries, which includes many of the developing countries, which are the most dependent upon foreign trade and the most vulnerable to major disturbances in the world economy. There have been sufficient steps in the direction of this evolution already to suggest that is not merely a chimerical danger. Controls on capital movements greatly proliferated during the currency disturbances of the past several years, especially while currencies were floating, and trade controls have been threatened.

There are two further risks. One is that anxiety about currencies arising from disturbances in the foreign exchange market may be contagious, and may reduce confidence by residents in their own currencies as well. This development could lead to a general erosion of confidence in nationally-managed money, a development of inflationary potential which national authorities alone might be unable to identify and correct.

The other risk is that a general deterioration of economic relations among countries will poison their relations in non-economic areas as well. Of all the areas of international relations, economics touches most directly on the majority of people. In an environment of mutual and retaliatory defensive action between nations, malign feelings toward "foreigners" are bound to develop, and in democracies such feelings can act as a powerful constraining factor on chief executives to pursue constructive courses of action, non-economic as well as economic, with other nations. Thus we believe a satisfactory and well-functioning international monetary system is a necessary if not alone a sufficient condition for harmonious international relations in all areas. During the period of 1971-1973 acrimony over monetary issues has risen alarmingly and we have flirted unwittingly with the high risk of undoing the vast gains of the preceding two decades in welding together at least the beginning of an international community among the non-communist industrial nations of the world.

V.

INTERIM PRIORITIES
AND TRANSITIONAL MEASURES

It will take several years, at best, to negotiate, formulate in legal terms, and ratify many of the proposed elements of the renovated system. Many untoward developments could occur during this transitional period. The experience of early 1973 is disquieting as regards the smooth functioning of the world economy without generally accepted financial rules. While the negotiations go forward, therefore, we need in addition to take steps to bridge the interim period and to establish the basis for the renovated system. These transitional measures are designated to restore a degree of calm and stability to currency and financial markets and to provide an environment of cooperation rather than contention in which the negotiations on longer-term measures can take place. We suggest five interrelated measures to be taken with a high sense of urgency:

1. coordination of intervention in exchange markets;

2. consolidation of some outstanding dollar balances;

3. enlargement of short-term lending facilities;

4. commitment to and control of the euro-currency market;

5. definition of a gold policy.

1. EXCHANGE MARKET INTERVENTION

Governments have repeatedly stated their belief that the exchange rates established in February 1973 were appropriate, with minor adjustments. Yet speculative pressures in exchange markets pushed exchange rates well away from that pattern, and also provided sharp and erratic day-to-day movements in rates. It would not be realistic to attempt to restore the February 1973 pattern of rates by central bank interventions in the market. But *the monetary authorities should state their unwillingness to see exchange rates battered about by momentary sentiments influencing the holders of volatile liquid funds. They should intervene in the markets, on a cooperative basis, in sufficient force to smooth out movements in exchange rates.* This kind of braking action, along with other interim measures discussed below, should be sufficient to influence private expectations about future movements in exchange rates, and to lead to an unwinding of the heavy speculative positions against the dollar.

We feel that the problem of "burden-sharing" in defending a currency which is depreciating has received more emphasis than it deserves. We support the rule of thumb that has apparently been adopted in the mid-1973 Basel agreements, that is, of splitting evenly between the debtor and the creditor central banks the costs of exchange losses that arise when borrowed funds are used in exchange market support operations. But profit and loss considerations should not play a large role in a central bank's attitude when such a basic economic variable as its exchange rate is at stake.

2. CONSOLIDATION OF FOREIGN EXCHANGE BALANCES

An important psychological depressant in the market for dollars has been the large outstanding official balances of dollars, balances that tripled in the two years 1971 and 1972 and grew by a further $13 billion in the first ten weeks of 1973, before the inauguration of floating. The act of floating itself demonstrated an unwillingness of many countries to add further to their dollar balances, even when they felt that the dollar had become an under-valued currency. This depressing factor can be relieved by steps to consolidate at least some of the dollar balances. (These arguments also apply, with less force, to outstanding official balances in sterling.)

Full consolidation in exchange for bancor, the revamped SDR, must await the longer-range reforms, including amendment of the Articles of the International Monetary Fund. But *some interim consolidation should be undertaken through a series of agreements between the United States and the largest creditor nations* under terms and conditions that are agreed among all the parties directly involved. The United States would provide an exchange guarantee on the balances in question, most appropriately by denominating them in units of account equivalent to the SDR. To this end, it would be essential to agree on the exact definition of the revamped SDR in the interim period, preferably along the lines we have recommended above, even before formal legislation can be obtained. Such agreement would permit use of the new unit of account. In addition, the United States would agree to amortize these balances over a suitably long period of time, chosen so that the interest and amortization payments together would not differ greatly from interest payments on outstanding dollar balances. Thus the amortization would not require unacceptably large U.S. surpluses in other transactions.

In exchange, creditor nations would accept a rate of interest appropriate to the guaranteed asset, and they would agree not to use the claims for any purpose, except under extreme balance of payments pressure, under which circumstances by agreement their liquidity might be restored.

Not all dollar balances should be handled in this way, for dollar holdings will remain during the transitional period the most usable form of international liquidity. But if a substantial share of the "overhang" could be funded, there would be salutory effects on market psychology. The amounts so funded could be taken over by the IMF substitution account when it began operation, and such conversion would of course restore the liquidity of the asset to the creditors.

3. SHORT-TERM LENDING FACILITIES

Market intervention, especially in the face of the massive movements of funds that became commonplace in the past two years, may require substantial amounts of foreign currencies. This obviously poses no problem for those countries that have amassed huge dollar reserves and who must intervene by selling dollars. But it does pose problems for the United States, which holds virtually no foreign exchange, and even for those countries with large dollar holdings who find they must intervene in the market for some other currency and do not want to disturb the market for dollars in the process.

To accommodate this possible need, large short-term credit facilities between central banks are necessary — an antecedent to the lender of last resort we have urged for the renovated international monetary system. We already have a network of central bank swap facilities, which perform this function at present. But *that network should be improved in three ways.* First, it should be further enlarged. The increase of the Federal Reserve bilateral swap arrangements to a total of $17 billion in July 1973 — with a maximum of $2 billion for a single currency — is not sufficient in a time when $2 billion can move into a given currency on a single day. Second, the network should be multilateralized, so that the actions of any pair of countries is under the surveillance of the community of nations, but not in such a way as to impede the speed of providing credits when necessary. Furthermore, credit facilities should be made available to other leading countries, as they already have been to some degree within the European Community. The arrangements should be designed to merge smoothly into the IMF lender-of-last-resort facility to be created as part of the longer-run renovation of the system. Third, a more systematic process should be established for extending credits that are not reversed through market forces in a relatively short period of time. These credits should become eligible for the consolidation arrangements discussed above, if necessary accompanied by any adjustment measures that may be necessary to prevent continuing calls on credit by a single country.

4. SURVEILLANCE OF THE EURO-CURRENCY MARKET

The euro-currency market is a much maligned feature of the international monetary system as it has evolved in the past decade. Many of the disturbances of the past few years have been attributed to it. But in fact the euro-currency market is itself a symptom of some of those same forces that are responsible for the disturbances — national disequilibria combined with greatly increased mobility of capital. And the euro-currency market has served the positive function of providing a genuine international market for money and credit that can readily and at low cost mobilize the savings of the world and channel them to productive investors. It represents the healthy beginning of a restoration of a true international capital market.

At the same time, there can be little doubt that the presence of the euro-currency market has made it easier to move funds from one currency to another on a massive scale than would have been possible in its absence; and there can also be little doubt that the rapid and largely uncontrolled growth of the euro-currency market has become a source of uneasiness in financial circles and among large holders of currencies. In the absence of outside review and standards for euro-banks, it may be that the standards of credit-worthiness applied to borrowers have declined markedly in the face of growing competition among participants in the market, raising the spectre of an old-fashioned collapse of the pyramid of credit that has developed in this new banking system.

We believe that the euro-currency market has greater resiliency than pessimistic observers contend. But we also believe that growing uneasiness would be considerably allayed if *the leading central banks jointly declared their readiness to stand squarely behind the euro-currency mar-*

ket in the event of major withdrawals by depositors. The commitment itself would help to obviate the need to honor it. In addition, the leading central banks should announce their intention, jointly and in cooperation, to study carefully the books of banks participating in the euro-currency market, holding out the possibility that some limits might be placed either on the asset side or on the liability side of their balance sheets if that were found to be desirable — limits analogous to reserve requirements or lending constraints typically found in domestic banking systems. This action would reinforce the salutory psychological impact of the commitment to stand behind the market in time of crisis, and by putting banks on notice that joint control was possible would itself introduce a new cautionary dimension into lending and borrowing decisions.

5. GOLD POLICY

The price of gold has evoked an attention out of all proportion to its real importance. We have already made clear our belief that new reserves have to be created by joint decisions in the form of bancor and not in the form of national currencies. Establishing an official higher price of gold would clearly be inconsistent with our view that bancor should constitute the principal reserve asset, increasing in importance over time. Indeed, we look eventually to the gradual abandonment of gold as an official monetary medium, although no doubt some gold will continue to be officially held as a contingency reserve, just as other real commodities are stockpiled by several countries today.

However, the day of the monetary unimportance of gold is still some time away. In the meantime, gold indisputably does attract attention in financial circles. *We believe an action consonant with our long-run objectives and at the same time advancing the interim aim of calming markets would be the coordinated and joint sale of official gold into private markets.* Such sales would require suppression of the March 1968 agreement to separate official from private gold transactions on the selling side. Sales should not aim to depress the market price greatly, but if moderate sales did so, that would be welcome. In recent years, the purchase of gold has seemed to provide a foolproof way to increase wealth. The official sale of gold, without a predetermined price, would interject much uncertainty into the gold market and would thus encourage funds to shift back to other assets and would help to restore confidence in currencies.

Official sales of gold would raise questions about the treatment of any discrepancy in price between the present official price and the market sales price. By their own testimony, central banks do not generally need additional reserves. The sales into private markets, other things being equal, would have a deflationary impact on the world economy by reducing purchasing power in private hands. We believe that the "capital gains" of central banks on gold sales would represent an attractive source, during the transitional period, of development assistance. The amounts could be consequential: sales of $3 billion in official gold could possibly raise twice that on the private market. Gold sales would represent a fiscally sound way to raise financial assistance, preferable in this respect to a link between SDR-creation and development assistance such as has been discussed by the Committee of Twenty. Still better, of course, would be a contributory system based on agreed principles of taxation in the rich countries of the world, but as a practical matter that falls well outside the transitional period we are now discussing. Gold sales in an agreed total amount could be apportioned among all countries for which gold accounted, say, for more than 10 percent of total reserves, in proportion to their excess holdings.

These five steps, taken together, represent concrete actions to bring the international monetary system back under control and, even more important, to do it in a way that indicates the willingness of the leading countries of the non-communist world to work together in a joint enterprise beneficial to all.

THE CRISIS OF

INTERNATIONAL COOPERATION

François Duchêne
DIRECTOR
International Institute of Strategic Studies
London

Kinhide Mushakoji
DIRECTOR
Institute of International Relations For Advanced Studies on Peace and Development in Asia
Tokyo

Henry D. Owen
DIRECTOR
Foreign Policy Studies Program The Brookings Institution
Washington

33

Table of Contents

34

I. THE CRISIS OF INTERNATIONAL COOPERATION

Economic and technological progress is now posing problems for mankind that dwarf those which led to the catastrophes of the first half of the century. The rate of productive growth, worldwide, has, in the past generation, reached an average about twice as high as in the most advanced regions alone in any previous comparable length of time. Electronic communications are thrusting ever closer together communities which have, throughout history, developed their social patterns, political institutions and cultural outlooks in relative isolation. This acceleration of the industrial revolution, encompassing virtually the whole world, has had immense effects. It is creating intense strains between societies with highly diverse traditions, perspectives, and needs. It is fueling the growing social aspirations which take different forms in different places, from the revolt of the young against materialism in "post-industrial" societies to the hunger for goods and equality in poorer ones. Moreover, the advances of industry and urbanism, especially in wealthier communities, are such that the capacity of the planet to accommodate the accelerating demand for resources and the growing degradation of the environment is for the first time being plausibly called into question. As if all this were not enough, Man's capacity to destroy his creations has also increased by several orders of magnitude: the discovery of nuclear fission and fusion has multiplied the destructive power of Man's "infernal machines" by ten thousand times.

All these developments call for a change in the habits and outlook of humanity for which little has prepared it. They also call for changes in the structures of decision-making, which are not adapted to the requirements of a common future. A world which has reached current levels of interdependence and is condemned by technological and economic progress to still more complex relationships in future, must devise new forms of common management. This is crucial if technical progress is to provide not chaos and injustice but a wider and deeper civility. The dangers of failing to adapt social, political and economic policy to industrial and technological change have been demonstrated at least twice this century. The generation that blundered into the

First World War failed to realise that industrial power had changed war from an eighteenth-century luxury, which may have marginally reduced the strain on scarce food supplies, into a machine for wholesale murder. The next generation, between the wars, immensely aggravated, if it did not actually create, the Great Depression. In both cases, confusion about the needs of modern interdependence, at least as much as deliberate policy, produced disaster.

If the postwar period offers a striking contrast, this has been at least partly because the lessons of prewar failures bit deeply into the consciousness of statesmen. The governments of major powers made unprecedented commitments to the joint international management of their common problems. The deliberate collective pursuit of policies of economic growth has probably been as responsible as nuclear weaponry itself for the remarkable paradox that the cold war has been for the advanced industrial societies a time of relative peace and prosperity without parallel, of economic "miracles," a *belle epoque.* Even the less developed countries, the underprivileged two-thirds of mankind, have been able as a result of this economic buoyancy to keep alive their aspirations to share one day in the benefits of affluence. It is this progress that provides the basis for hopes that the coming crisis of industrial civilisation may yet be creatively mastered in the interests of humanity as a whole.

The realisation of these hopes depends in large measure on whether mankind can muster the political will to manage common problems collectively. The outlook is uncertain.

The immediate postwar efforts to make the United Nations the focus for worldwide cooperation foundered on the schism between revolutionary and evolutionary states. The nuclear inhibition has moderated this split — driving the superpowers towards contractual arrangements that ratify their strategic parity. But this management of what has been called the "central balance" is itself very limited. It is confined to the superpowers; it does not end the rivalry between them; it does not of itself create (though it encourages) forms of cooperation which reach out towards other fields and other countries; and it does not touch the problems which the new technologies pose, and will increasingly pose, for all societies, irrespective of their social and political systems.

Cooperation between rich and poor has also been woefully inadequate. The postwar period has seen the development of a network of agencies of great potential — the World Bank; the regional banks; the specialised agencies of the United Nations, from FAO and WHO to the United Nations Organisation for Cooperation on Trade and Development (UNCTAD). But the fact is that the rich industrial nations of the West have, on the whole, made too little effort to intensify their cooperation with the less developed countries. It is hard to avoid the conclusion that once empire or cold war no longer demanded it, most rich societies lost interest in the poor. There are signs of change. Japanese and Western European aid to developing nations is growing; external private investment in these areas is on the increase; and exports of their manufactures have been expanding at the rate of 15% annually in recent years. Slowly and painfully, the beginnings of a kind of trade unionism are also developing among the less developed countries. But these changes are not enough.

Interdependence between rich industrial societies is necessarily more intense than between less developed ones, each of which tends to be isolated by its poverty. In addition, cooperation between mainly market economies is more permeating and socially all-embracing than between centrally planned state systems: in market economies, relations depend on the myriad decentralized activities of groups and individuals and penetrate far more widely and deeply than even modern governments can reach. As a result, international cooperation has developed furthest among the advanced industrial societies, especially North America, Japan and Western Europe. If collective action were to fail in this crucial area of interdependence, what confidence could there be that it would succeed in others where links are more tenuous?

There is every reason to expect that cooperation between the industrial democracies will be just as central to the future world system as it has been to world peace for the past generation. To be sure, there are great differences of power, geography, outlook, and interests between North America, Japan and Western Europe. Nevertheless, their collective behaviour must largely create the framework of opportunity for the world economy. The problems of money, trade, investment, resources, and peace cannot be creatively tackled unless they cooperate. This would be dramatically evident if they failed: rivalry and protectionism between them could constrain opportunities for everyone else. In short, international cooperation generated by the advanced industrial democracies has reached a crossroads. The great increase in the interdependence of the advanced industrial societies has generated new economic and social phenomena which cannot be dealt with through the old prescriptions.

THE CHANGING BALANCE OF POWER

a) *Security*. The shift from the Manichean bipolar confrontation of East and West of the cold war to a politically mobile, multipolar world is in full swing. The fear of nuclear confrontation has increasingly constrained the rivalry of the superpowers during the past twenty years — leading first to great caution and then to an awareness of their potential common interests. The schism between the two great Communist powers, the Soviet Union and China, has removed the bogey of a monolithic Communist world, enabling the United States to initiate a diplomacy of manoeuvre and balance. The gradual revelation that the problems of advanced industrial societies, including socialist ones, cannot be finessed by revolution, has turned hostility between East and West into an awareness, however wary, that cooperation may in future be possible as well as desirable. At the same time, the ambiguities of the cold war persist in many ways. The superpowers are still competing for political and military power, the Sino-Soviet schism might veer to outright conflict, and Soviet-U.S. strategic parity raises doubts about America's security guarantees both to Japan and NATO which could lead to destabilizing nuclear proliferation. The greater flexibility which now exists in the "strategic triangle" between the United States, the Soviet Union and China has somewhat reduced the urgency of America's concern to buttress its partners, Japan and Europe, in the "economic triangle": the world balance now seems more able to take care of itself. Moreover, the desire to retain freedom of manoeuvre at the strategic level encourages the U.S. to pursue a unilateral style of diplomacy. While this pays off in dealing with "limited adversaries" like the Soviet Union and China, it tends to create doubts as to where U.S. priorities lie and to inject suspicion into partnership relations. "Nixon shocks" are no breeders of confidence.

The behaviour of the U.S. affects the attitudes of its partners, in their turn. The first reaction to new doubts may actually be to increase their sense of dependence on the United States. In Europe, fear of American troop withdrawals has heightened the stress on the American link, to the point where the United States has been tempted to use the military needs of its allies as a bargaining point for economic concessions. This can, however, create a sense of inequity and poison the relationship as a whole. So a further stage is conceivable, for instance in the case of Japan, where the ally may consider itself less beholden and shift to a non-committal or neutral position and even acquire its own nuclear arms. Thus, whereas security factors at first powerfully reinforced all the industrially advanced societies' commitment to economic internationalism, they have now introduced into it an element if not of contradiction at least of permanent ambiguity.

b) *Economics.* As a result, the economic patterns of cooperation must in future justify themselves much more on their own isolated merits than in the past. But here, too, conditions have changed. The United States is no longer willing to manage the system without close attention to strict short-term reciprocity. The dollar deficit, at first deliberately incurred, proved in the period after 1960 to be highly intractable to the limited remedial measures America was ready to undertake. Its partners now have vast hoards of dollars, which central banks keep because the dollar is the world's reserve currency but which are an embarrassment because it is also a national currency.

Moreover the revival of Europe and Japan has profoundly changed the system. Japan, which has long been the most dynamic economy in the world, has now become the third greatest economic power and a major industrial competitor of the United States. The spectacular impact of Japan's exports on highly visible sectors of America's economy like synthetic fibres, colour television, and cars has prompted a protectionist revival in American opinion and raised questions in the minds of some Americans about how Japan can be related to the more slowly growing economies of the other industrial powers.

As for the enlarged European Community, it is now the world's second market and much the greatest international trading group, handling almost 40% of world trade. Its creation changed the economic balance of power against the United States, as was evident in the Kennedy Round negotiations to cut trade barriers in the mid-1960's. The policies pursued by the Europeans in their quest for political unity have also created problems. The Common Market has, almost spontaneously and without deliberation, tended to generate spheres of economic influence, particularly among the Mediterranean and African states, which seek association agreements with it in order to preserve their advantages of access. The result has been to raise fears of neo-colonial *chasses gardées* between the great economic powers — Europe, the United States and Japan — and the regions to the south of them, Africa, Latin America and south-east Asia. Were such a development to occur, it would be a disaster. It would arouse among the ex-colonial peoples fears for their independence and divide those that seek association from those that do not. It could also encourage beggar-my-neighbour relations between the rich and lead to a scramble for dear or scarce raw materials or fuels, like oil.

Faced with these challenges, the United States has started to behave more like an ordinary member of the system, entering into competitive devaluations, placing unilateral restraints on imports and more recently exports, and generally using the bargaining power inherent in its monetary, economic, and political strength — and even in its overseas troop deployments — in efforts to obtain concessions from its partners. These manoeuvres have been only partially successful, but they have shown that once the United States ceases to provide necessary backing, the system must either be reformed or founder in a rebirth of economic nationalism. Simply stated, the problem is a structural one. The international system, which depended heavily on U.S. leadership and sustenance, now requires a truly common management to which North America, the European Community and Japan must — in view of their large economic power — make a special contribution. For the United States, this means a sense of loss of power because decisions have to be shared more than in the past; for the European Community and Japan it means a sense of burden, because new responsibilities have to be assumed and, in some cases, paid for. For all three, the shift from a leadership system to one of genuine collective management, involving not only the three main industrial market economies but other countries as well, calls for what Robert Frost called "the courage to be new."

QUALITATIVE CHANGE

a) *Interdependence* is nothing new — its existence was implicit in prewar failures — but its present scale certainly is. Phenomena indicative of interactions across national frontiers have grown during the past generation even faster than output as a whole. Trade between the major economies, for instance, has increased about 8% annually, against an average annual growth of the global economy of about 5%. International production by integrated multinational companies has risen even faster, about 10% per year; over a fifth of the industrial output of market economy countries is now controlled by corporations which plan their investment, their fiscal transfers, their use of production capacity, their sales policies, etc., on a transnational basis. Air travel, symbolic of the increasingly global activities of elites, has grown even faster — about 15% yearly. The exponential rate of growth of

40

the Eurodollar market and of funds which are not effectively under national controls is another mark of this main trend.

It is difficult to imagine the ties thus created being unwound into national or regional self-sufficiencies. The system that has engendered these transnational links was, after all, set up to meet powerful aspirations for full employment, mass consumption, free travel, and even free access to ideas. The prosperity of Japan and the European Community is bound up with that of the general international system, the core of which is their relationship with the United States and each other. Though the United States is apparently far less dependent on its foreign economic relations — they account for a mere 4-5% of the U.S. GNP — all its major corporations are deeply committed to foreign investment and markets, its balance of payments heavily depends on their income, its people expect freedom to consume foreign goods, its industry needs foreign fuels and raw materials, and their relative cost and weight in the economy is bound to grow. The whole dynamic of business activity is moving toward greater, not less, international involvement.

At the same time, in an interdependent world, shocks are transmitted from one society to another with great intensity and speed, without each government acknowledging, or perhaps appreciating, its own role in the vicious circle of transnational disturbance. Behind collective appearances, the early postwar system was one of relative isolation. Japan and Western Europe entertained bilateral relations primarily with the United States, whose strength was such that it did not feel the strain. Now, the situation is quite different. Trade flows can change rapidly and massively, and even in the United States certain sectors are powerfully affected by these changes. The sheer amount of trade between members of the European Community is such that one country, even Germany, cannot isolate itself, say, from neighbouring inflation. Central banks trying to restrain internal booms by raising interest rates find capital funds flocking to profit from the better returns and so reinforcing domestic inflation. The list of interactions which produce situations no one has consciously desired is almost endless, and qualitatively new items are coming to swell it even now. For years the United States has been trying to increase its farm markets in Europe and Japan to help balance its payments and the soyabean has been among products spearheading the campaign. But sudden shortage in the United States in 1973 produced an export ban, to increase supplies and damp down prices in America, so increasing the problems of shortage and inflationary pressures in countries that import soya and shifting the burden onto them. This kind of autarkic reaction could become increasingly prominent, now that the problems of scarcity are being added to those of abundance.

In a world where economic interchanges are increasingly international but responsibilities are national, each government, and even more each legislature, experience the new development as a loss of control. In its efforts to ward off external complications a government tends, at least in part, to take defensive measures — which export them back to the outside world, that is, to the other participants in the system. Not surprisingly, the level of confrontation rises to the detriment of the general interest. This loss of national sovereignty, painful to each society and government individually, must lead in one of two directions in an interdependent system which is unlikely to break up. Either there will be progress toward international cooperation or, dealing with the symptoms rather than the under-lying disturbances, national governments will seek to exploit the so-called "asymmetries" of the situation. Less euphemistically, this means that governments will exploit each situation with an eye to the maximum gain for themselves even if it means loss for others and the system as a whole. This is the crude power politics of an interdependent age, carrying the seeds of domination and inequality between societies.

A complicating problem is the increasing involvement of public authorities, national and regional, in the whole economic process. In Europe, many governments now channel almost 40% of the GNP through their budgets and by the 1980's the proportions are expected to rise towards 50%. In Japan and North America the proportions are lower but, as social demands become more insistent, they are also rising. Regional policies, subsidies to particular industries, government markets, measures to protect the environment or to humanise the assembly line, policies to protect underprivileged groups or ones that have a particularly strong bargaining power, all these impinge, or can impinge, on international economic relations. As the partial replacement of Economic Man by the Welfare Society progresses, there must be some collective arena for confronting the consequences of the economic and social policies of national governments as they affect, or are affected by, their partners.

b) *Social and Political Change.* These problems are compounded by the revival of social turbulence after a generation of exceptional domestic quiet. For a time, the blossoming of the mass consumption society

42

seemed to still social turmoil in and between industrial market economy countries. This social quiescence now seems to have been considerably eroded.

This is partly due to the impact of interdependence, which has stirred up protectionism — for example, in American labour; partly to progress itself, for instance with farmers who feel its victims; and partly to the emergence of new self-assertive groups, such as skilled workers in many industries. But, over and above all these, there has developed a new social climate, the feeling that all problems *can* be solved, so that it is intolerable if they are not. A new self-assertiveness demands that policies should be related to the individual as the measure of his rights instead of to the state as the measure of his obligations or to the market as the measure of his earning power.

Within societies, this trend has led to competition between different groups, including strong industrial and labour lobbies. It has also led to implicit competition between societies, of which the export of inflation is a symptom. It has, not least, had a great deal to do with the growing indifference of advanced industrial societies, in practice if not in theory, to the far worse problems of poverty of the Third World. Indignant lobbies within the developed societies have far more political clout than indignant ones outside.

The increased role of governments in production and welfare adds to the problem: in the past, the fortunes and misfortunes of producers could be ascribed to the abstract and impersonal forces of the market; today they are more and more traceable to deliberate governmental choices, and to that extent are politicised, both at home and in the international arena. As a result, increasing governmental centralisation produces a paradoxical weakening of authority in the face of the ever increasing range of articulate and assertive lobbies. Societies become internally more turbulent and externally less responsive to each others' needs. Charity beginning at home is associated with national truculence in dealings with others, even though nationalism as an ideology of the major industrial powers has probably reached its lowest ebb since the French Revolution.

In the first postwar enthusiasm to reconstruct the world, the preoccupation of leaders of the industrial countries was with creating a better system, on the assumption that the general interest mattered more than relative gains and losses between partners. Today there has been a reversion to the attitude which pays attention to relative rather than global benefits, suggesting a general loss of perspective. This may be linked to the revival of traditional state structures which, in Europe and Japan, had been rocked to their foundations by the war. The U.S. case is a special one. The United States emerged after the war from a period of isolationism and domestic reform, and sought to reshape the world in the mould of the New Deal. But the practice of world power has cooled America's crusading ardour, as evidenced by concepts of Realpolitik which have bloomed in the academic community and in Washington in recent years and the prestige of political theories based on bargaining between "adversaries."

Given all these pressures, it is not surprising that the postwar system of the advanced industrial democracies should now be in crisis. The whole situation is finely balanced between contradictory trends and opposing forces, and political goodwill cannot be taken for granted as in the past.

A MORE VULNERABLE WORLD

Although the balance of nuclear prudence makes war much less likely between major powers, the world may well be moving towards a more vulnerable era. As the planet grows more crowded and progress moves from an extensive to a more intensive phase, the competition for advantage risks becoming more acute. Currently such issues as fishing rights off Iceland are still treated with the regard for public opinion and due political behaviour rather than of interstate relations in the past. But if nationalism on the high seas were to become the norm, this restraint could come to an abrupt stop. If one looks further ahead, disproportionate bargaining power may accrue to the few. World food production will be increasingly dependent on the capacity of a handful of large modern economies such as the United States, Canada and Australia to provide surpluses. The dependence of world activity on a few oil producers will grow, and the less developed countries could suffer most from a clash between these producers and the major industrial powers. Or in the fields of the more futuristic technologies — particularly those dependent on space, such as communications or weather control — the superpowers, particularly the United States, could well accentuate their lead over other societies. If the world is to be dominated by power politics, many societies will suffer, or fear that they are about to suffer, and, since security is a subjective matter, the insecurity of humanity will increase.

There are signs that the advanced democratic societies might be all too easily infected by such an international climate. There are a number of causes for this. One of them is the failure, or rather the disappointing fulfillment, of the utopian hopes of a generation ago. Revolutionary Communism has foundered in bureaucratic conservatism and Realpolitik; the non-industrial countries have seen the heady political liberation of the colonial peoples subside in poverty and a sense of economic victimisation; and even the more moderate expectations of Western social democracy have soured into distaste with the materialism of the mass consumption society. These hopes were attached to ostensibly "rational" secular ends; in fact, they masked a millenialism which re-emerged immediately after the End of Ideology. The fascination with nuclear Apocalypse, despite the actual and unprecedented retreat from adventure in great power politics, is rooted deep in the consciousness of an age which has produced movements like the hippies or playwrights like Samuel Beckett. There is a constant temptation in a world whose complexities defy common understanding to alienation and politically dangerous oversimplification. Moreover, these cultural forces have been matched by such mass social changes as the sudden depopulation of the land in every industrial country, or the appearance of large minorities of migrant workers, all of which encourage both radicalism and backlashes, alike favourable to extremist politicians.

II. TOWARD A COMMON APPROACH

WELFARE AND THE WORLD ECONOMY

In a complex world with many actors, new forces can only be controlled by a coherent view of the problems that one confronts. Today, more than ever before, a broad view of needs and consequent goals is a prerequisite of progress.

One dominant characteristic of society today is the shift in preoccupation from growth as a social policy in itself, to a belief in the need for more governmental effort to direct and shape growth — either as a result of social competition for wealth; or to meet particular regional, social or industrial needs; or to satisfy environmental priorities; or to deal with new constraints — such as in the supply of raw materials — in ways which societies accept as domestically just. This does not deny the value of growth; the majority of the world's peoples are still living at or near the subsistence level; and even in rich countries large minorities, of a fifth or more, live in poverty by local standards, and those just above the poverty level also aspire to higher living standards. Nor does it deny economic priorities: It is as important as ever to seek to open, and keep open, the international economy. But it is necessary to see this goal in new terms, if new priorities are to be served. From one point of view, inflation resulting from social competition has to be accommodated or controlled. From another, there is an analogy with the problem faced by the architects of the European Community when they set up their common market. With the opening up of a new European arena of economic interdependence, it became potentially impossible for each country to maintain its own domestic policies unless these were shared by the system as a whole. Domestic political priorities had to be reasserted at the new international level. The difficulty, then and now, is that priorities vary from country to country. Nevertheless, unless they can be at least partly reconciled in a positive way, it will be difficult to avoid a vicious circle in which either the uncoordinated international system breaks the capacity of each nation to control its environment or the nations break the system.

The Advanced Industrial Societies must reform their system on two levels in particular.

One is the monetary framework of the international economy. In many ways the world has outgrown the postwar monetary system and this has produced considerable confusion on the international exchange markets. A situation must not be allowed to evolve in which monetary developments undermine the confidence in prosperity and the economic optimism built up over two decades. The immediate need is to improve the working of the present system of flexible exchange rates. Over the longer term, the monetary system must be consolidated on terms which satisfy three aims. One is to confirm sufficient flexibility in the system to allow for differential economic trends and policies from one country to another, but not so much as to lead to national self-sufficiency under a new guise. The second is to reinforce recent moves toward a managed international currency in ways which provide a new standard of value and a new capacity to deal with short-term capital movements. The third is to provide the less developed countries with the more abundant multilateral finance from the advanced industrial societies which they need.

Collective action has also become necessary at the level where new forms of control over production impinge on the international economy. This applies both to national economic policies and to such private transnational actors as the multinational corporations. In an intensely interdependent world, it is important not to allow national or private authorities to act without taking account of the inter-action between the societies involved and without recognising some responsibility for the distortions that they engender for everyone. Regional policies to maintain activity and employment in a backward or threatened area should not be carried to the point where subsidised competition creates similar social and industrial problems for others. On the other hand, experiments in social progress, such as attempts to humanise the manufacture of motorcars by breaking up the assembly line, should not be precluded by the fact that they may defy the laws of comparative costs, without some consideration of possible public policies to subsidise or otherwise encourage experiments. Similarly, multinational corporations should not be allowed to spread their tax loads irrespective of their economic and political consequences for individual host nations or the system as a whole. None of this calls for formal international controls, except perhaps as a last resort. It does, however, demand that governments should effectively confront the consequences of their national policies in the international arena, case by case, and take account in their domestic policies of their partners' preoccupations. As a recent study of these issues concluded: "If we want to domesticate the nascent anarchic ways of the makers of foreign economic policy, we must domesticate the international economy itself."*

The Less Developed Countries. Reciprocal accountability as the basic principle of cooperation should apply equally to relations between the advanced industrial democracies and the less developed countries. The less developed countries are the guilty conscience of the rich, though in practice the rich have listened to their conscience as little as they dared because of competition between underprivileged groups at home and the much poorer poor abroad. But newly emerging forces will raise the price of such indifference. Developed countries' industries, which are already beginning to manufacture products in developing countries to benefit from lower costs and advantages of access, will become so many future hostages. Monetary and trade negotiations will be difficult to prosecute successfully without the cooperation of developing countries — as will efforts to reduce worldwide pollution and preserve global resources.

For these and other reasons, what will increasingly be needed in the period ahead is real cooperation between the industrial and pre-industrial societies. It should be based on the projection of latent common interests and joint activities arising out of them, and involve not only the transfer of capital but also the sharing of markets and skills in production and distribution, and help with infrastructure and technical assistance of all kinds. This approach, going beyond aid to cooperation, needs to inform all relations with less developed countries. It is clear that most less developed countries are determined to be helped only to help themselves. Attempts to establish spheres of influence through investments or trade are likely to boomerang. They will not only draw the hostility of the more vigorous LDC's; they will also divide the advanced industrial societies. The approach then must be multilateral.

TOWARD A "PLANETARY HUMANISM"

In the last resort, a "planetary humanism," to use Zbigniew Brzezinski's phrase, offers the only common goals for societies as diverse as those of the advanced industrial democracies. The colonisation of the oceans and space, the impact of new technologies, and the control of the environment and the biosphere in an overwhelmingly industrial, urban, and crowded world will all create new opportunities for conflict or

*"The Community and the Changing World Economic Order," by Theo Peeters and Wolfgang Hager, in *A Nation Writ Large? Foreign Policy Problems before the European Community,* edited by Max Kohnstamm and Wolfgang Hager (Macmillan, 1973).

cooperation. There is no doubt of the divisive potential of such issues, for example, between the industrial powers anxious to reduce "pollution" and the pre-industrial ones anxious to produce more. It is all the more important, therefore, to reinforce the frameworks of cooperation that already exist. Once it was thought that economic needs were essentially divisive: Cecil Rhodes, Lenin, and Hitler all shared that view. Postwar cooperation has shown its essential falsity. It is clear now that whatever the conflicts over fair shares, all have an interest in the system's working well. In a crowded world, the goals of planetary humanism must be sought through the rules, institutions, and contracts of common management.

III. Trilateral Cooperation

A broad vision of goals is necessary, but it must be complemented by procedures which give a sense of participation in a common effort to overcome common problems. Most current difficulties are due less to the issues in themselves — they are manageable — than to the problem of making the general interest emerge in a period of confusion. In the metaphor often used by Jean Monnet, negotiators usually confront one another across the table when in fact they should sit on the same side of it and confront the problems on the other side.

Despite its recent statements regarding trilateralism, the United States Government has preferred in the last few years to deal bilaterally with individual European governments and Japan, and to centralise relations on itself, as in the past, believing that this maximised its bargaining power and prolonged its leadership. The Europeans and Japanese fell in with this. The Europeans not yet having achieved the unity to speak with one voice, individual European governments are fearful that their particular views will be submerged in the general negotiation and prefer to deal directly with the United States, a pattern of behaviour which encourages them to see their context as essentially Atlantic. Some European governments also prefer to deal bilaterally with the United States and Japan because they fear that U.S. influence would be dominant in any trilateral arrangement. Japanese governments also have preferred to deal bilaterally with America, and use a pragmatic form of policy-making which studiously avoids explicit statements in order to build up the domestic consensus; they are reluctant to take initiatives unless they must. And the cool reactions which greeted Prime Minister Tanaka's recent discussions of trilateralism in Europe have probably tended to discourage future Japanese initiatives in this direction.

But the drawbacks of bilateralism are great. It is not surprising that the Japanese and Europeans, though of great potential importance to each other, both in themselves and in the effect they have on America, have very little sense of each other or their potential role together in the international system. The necessary development of a Europe able to speak with a single voice is made more difficult. And the United States is encouraged to underrate its partners' adaptations to a changing context. It sees itself all too easily as the only power with an adequate world view, an attitude which buttresses its unilateralism and desire to maintain the privileges of leadership, even when it is less and less able to exercise leadership responsibilities by itself.

The worst dangers of bilateralism are psychological: it always excludes someone. The feeling on the part of any nation that it has been left out, misinformed, or informed after the crucial moment of decision sows distrust and prepares further discord. This is a particular problem in view of the very different historical backgrounds of Japan and the Atlantic societies. It is natural that Japan should feel easily discriminated against by its newfound partners with a very different cultural tradition. It is also natural that there should be confusions of perspective to be taken into account. Japan's definition of what is "fair" assumes that latecomers have the right to be attributed a kind of "handicap" to make the game an equal one; the others feel that if there is any inequality, in economics at least, the boot is on the other foot. There are also differences in political style. Most (though not all) Europeans and Americans tend to formulate problems in specific terms and to subject them to universally applicable rules. The Japanese, with the instinctive unity of an island culture, keep situations fluid and revisable. These differences are surmountable, but to violate sensibilities can only complicate the task and divide what has only been newly joined. The problem is not limited to Japan. There are wide differences of perception between Europe and the United States about such issues as social justice and the role of governments in the economy — at home and abroad.*

Such political, diplomatic and psychological problems need careful handling. It is true that there is a community of the advanced industrial states in the sense that failure to agree on common issues will be detrimental to all of them and to their partners in the wider world. But it is also true that relative gains and losses to each party need not seem the same. It will not invariably be self-evident to all that global perspectives are more relevant than regional or national ones. Nor will it be recognised without question that some groups should bear the real or fancied costs of general benefits for all. In an intricate situation such as this, strong representation must be given to the general interest, while it should be accepted that harmony at all levels cannot be consistently attained. What can be hoped for is forms of consultation which do not merely avoid fractures in cooperation between the trilateral partners but positively promote a view of the general interest and so help them to formulate policies "from the same side of the table." The minimum is that governments should not present their partners and be

*See the Table on Page 55 for the very different images of each other and the situation entertained by the United States, the European Community and Japan.

allowed to get away with unilateral or bilateral faits accomplis which are irreversible. This may not be easy to accomplish because governments are likely to transgress precisely when they feel the most pressure to do so.

Promoting a positive awareness of the general interest is not susceptible to governmental rules or a high degree of institutionalisation for a variety of reasons.

One is the existence of a variety of international functional bodies, such as GATT and OECD, which are the right places for formal cooperation, precisely because they are functional, and therefore include all the interested parties, trilateral or not. To cut across them with trilateral bodies would be divisive — and is in practice impossible because it would oversimplify the diverse interests and relationships of the advanced industrial democracies themselves.

A second reason is equally basic: The problem is not to implement a consensus on policies, but to create one. Such a consensus existed among the postwar leaders, who had gone through the harrowing experiences of the 1930's and the war. Today the task is infinitely harder because the immediate past is a record of relative success and there has been no comparable failure — or even experience — which might induce a consensus on problems which are mostly new. In such conditions, the formal launching of ideas on an official stage would be a mistake: it would expose them prematurely to a mode of formal bargaining between governments without laying any of the political bases for their acceptance. What is most urgently needed is an informal process of collective self-education to generate the joint perspectives from which joint policies can spring. Such a process must be public, creating awareness of the need for international initiatives on international problems.

Of course, the final aim must be collective action by governments and eventually it should be possible to formalise consultation among them. It might, for instance, be possible to conceive of an international Advisory Commission of, say, three internationally respected statesmen with sufficient prestige to state the general interest, clarify the political stakes, and pave the way for the domestic acceptance of concession and compromise. But the time for this has not yet come. Today, such formalisation is not the only nor even necessarily the best way to promote a consensus. Leadership in such matters cannot be limited to politicians and bureaucracies whose responsibilities are rooted in historic systems which are institutionally separate from one another, and who are therefore ill-prepared by their training and loyalties to deal with transnational issues. Leadership cannot be exercised without them, but it need not be generated by them alone. Private citizens also, with the freedom to look at international problems in terms of their impact upon the general interest and not as items of intergovernmental bargaining, should point to new opportunities and risks, and suggest new political directions.

It is in this spirit that the Trilateral Commission, with participants from North America, Japan and the European Community, has been set up to propose jointly considered contributions by their nations to the major international issues that confront mankind. The Trilateral Commission will consider and publish studies which illuminate these issues, and it will publish policy papers which reflect its members' views on, among other things, money, trade, resources, relations with the less developed countries and with the centrally planned societies. Studies prepared for the Trilateral Commission on the less developed countries will be prepared in consultation with non-governmental personalities from those countries.

This first report for the Commission constitutes a preliminary statement of some of the considerations which led to the formation of the Trilateral Commission and some of the principles which will be relevant to the Commission's work, now and in the years to come. Since the work of the Trilateral Commission will essentially constitute a joint search for new political perspectives and opportunities, this statement will be kept under review as conditions change.

Creation of the Trilateral Commission reflects an awareness that the present moment is of very great importance for the future of mankind. The bipolar leadership system of the cold war is diffusing into what may be the first truly global political system, with many actors playing significant parts at different levels.

The nations of the world are not used to competitive interdependence, and tend to relapse into traditional confrontation. The danger in these circumstances is that change may lead to anarchy and anarchy to repressive national and international politics. Most highly evolved civilian communities are unlikely to lose their balance if they are open to a healthy outside world. But if the international context is itself unhealthy and many countries are thrown off balance together, it becomes infinitely more difficult for any one of them to re-establish its equilibrium and a vicious circle of instability and hatreds may be set off, leading to catastrophe.

If, on the other hand, the advanced industrial societies succeed in advancing from previous forms of nation-state cooperation to new forms of collective cooperation, they will have created a framework to deal with the essential problems of the next decades. These include the maintenance of open societies at home; the gradual breaking down of the still existing frontiers between East, West and the poor; and the tackling of controlled growth in a *"monde fini,"* as Valéry called it, where resources and the ecosystem have to be respected in order to be exploited for the benefit of mankind. If those conditions are met, trilateral cooperation will be a building block of a more harmoniously ordered international system, not a bloc as such. It will help to turn what Marion Doenhoff has called the "technical peace" of nuclear inhibition into a "political peace" of accepted international process. In so doing, the partners can give themselves a political purpose no longer provided by growth alone: at the further end of cold war, they can afford civilianisation without fear.

TABLE: TRILATERAL PERCEPTIONS*

		View Concerning U. S.	View Concerning E. C.	View Concerning Japan	Extra-Trilateral World Priorities
U.S. VIEW	(E):	Global responsibility of $. Deficit due to US contribution to Free World security & development.	Danger of closed regionalism. Euro-$ monetary imbalance.	Unrealistic strength of ¥. Too much restriction on own market & too much aggressivity in US market.	(E): Latin America.
	(P):	Tripolar balance priority & US leadership role in Free World.	North Atlantic cooperation indispensable for Free World.	Should play a political role in accordance w. economic power in cooperation w. USA.	(P): USSR & China.
	(M):	US nuclear guarantee plus Free World countries' contribution to security.	Increased security responsibility needed as well as cooperation with US nuclear and ACD policy.	Insufficient sharing of security burden in Asia.	(M): USSR.
E.C. VIEW	(E):	Dominant economy. Economic & technological gaps; the American challenge.	EC integration stabilising factor for world economy.	Same as the US.	(E): Africa.
	(P):	N. Atlantic hegemony questioned.	East-West European affairs' key role in the world.	Economic diplomacy with no relevant role in high politics.	(P): Eastern European countries.
	(M):	Nuclear bipolar balance. US presence in Europe necessary for EC	European regional security.	No interest.	(M): Same as above.
JAPAN VIEW	(E):	Same as Europe, plus fear of protectionistic reactions.	Profit from integration, danger of closed market. Europe-centered. Not enough interest in Asia.	Deserving special treatment. Still growing economy.	(E): Asia, China & USSR.
	(P):	Special US-Japanese relations.		Necessity to cope w. extreme dependence on foreign countries.	(P): China & USSR.
	(M):	Pressure on Japan for burden sharing unreasonable.	Indifferent.	Limited to self-defence.	(M): —

E = Economic; P = Political; M = Military.

*Prepared by Kinhide Mushakoji

55

A TURNING POINT IN

NORTH-SOUTH ECONOMIC RELATIONS

Richard N. Gardner
*Professor of Law
and International
Organization
Columbia University*
New York

Saburo Okita
*President
Overseas Economic
Cooperation Fund*
Tokyo

B. J. Udink
*Former Minister
for Aid to
the Developing
Countries*
The Netherlands

Table of Contents

A TURNING POINT IN
NORTH-SOUTH ECONOMIC RELATIONS

There are critical turning points in history when the lives and fortunes of large numbers of human beings hang upon the outcome of decisions taken by a small handful of national leaders. We have reached such a turning point in relations between the advanced industrialized countries of Europe, North America and Japan, on the one hand, and the developing countries of the Middle East, Africa, Asia and Latin America on the other.

The oil embargo — the fourfold increase in oil prices — the higher costs and severe shortages of food and fertilizer — the unprecedented concurrence of acute inflation and recession throughout the industrialized world — these events have gravely strained the tenuous fabric of international economic relations. In particular, they have detonated an explosion in North-South economic relations that has been building up for years. While demonstrating more clearly than ever before the interdependence of developed and developing nations, they have also provided a new stimulus to the advocates of economic nationalism and of confrontation by economic blocs. In short, they have raised the most troubling questions about the world's ability to manage its interdependence through peaceful cooperation.

We believe the time has come for new policies and new actions by the governments of the Trilateral region in their relations with the developing countries. Interdependence is now a persuasive fact as well as a convenient slogan. The developing countries need the aid, technology, know-how and markets of the Trilateral world. The Trilateral countries increasingly need the developing countries as sources of raw materials, as export markets, and, most important of all, as constructive partners in the creation of a workable world order. In our approach to this subject we reject any idea of a "rich man's club" forming defensive alliances against the poor. On the contrary, we seek a new international economic order based on cooperation between developed and developing countries, corresponding to the new balance of economic and political power, and responsive to growing demands for welfare and justice. We are convinced that an international economic system cannot successfully endure unless both rich and poor countries feel they have a stake in it.

The crisis in North-South relations has two vital aspects that require immediate responses from governments of the Trilateral region:

The *first* aspect is the desperate plight of nearly one billion people in some thirty resource-poor developing countries whose governments cannot pay the increased bills for oil, food, fertilizer, and other products. According to the World Bank, at least $3 billion in extra concessional aid must be found for these countries in 1974-75 to avoid economic disaster. This first report of the Trilateral Commission Task Force on Relations with Developing Countries offers a plan to make this sum available through an extraordinary act of cooperation between the countries of the Trilateral region and the oil producing countries.

The *second* aspect is the urgent necessity of a general restructuring of the international institutions governing North-South economic relations. We propose to deal with the extremely broad and complex questions involved in this restructuring in a later report to be issued early in 1975. But we take the occasion of this first report to offer some general considerations about economic relations between North and South which should be reflected in any reformed institutional structure.

I

Only last year, the World Bank estimated that the developing world as a whole would be able to sustain the 6% rate of growth which was the minimum objective of the Second United Nations Development Decade. This relatively hopeful prospect has been shattered by the following developments:

— the quadrupling of oil prices has added about $10 billion a year to the import bills of the non-oil-producing developing countries;

— the increase of food and fertilizer costs has added another $5 billion a year to the import bills of these countries;

— there has been a steep rise in the prices of other raw materials and manufactured goods imported by developing countries;

— the general economic slowdown in the industrialized world is reducing the foreign exchange earnings flowing to developing countries from merchandise exports, tourism and workers' remittances.

To grasp the full meaning of these events for the developing countries it needs only to be noted that the extra $15 billion that these countries must now pay for oil, food and fertilizer is almost double the $7-8 billion in total development assistance coming to them each year from all the industrialized countries of the Trilateral region.

In terms of their capacity to absorb these severe economic blows, the non-oil-producing developing countries can be divided into two categories:

1. There are countries like Mexico, Brazil, Turkey and Malaysia, which enjoy substantial foreign exchange reserves, high prices for their exports or ready access to capital markets. These countries can take care of themselves without additional concessional aid. However, some of these countries will require additional short or medium-term borrowing facilities from international institutions to enable them to maintain their development programs during the 1974-75 period.

2. There are the resource-poor, low-income developing countries that lack large foreign exchange reserves, buoyant export prospects, or the ability to service credit on commercial or near-commercial terms. This group of countries — sometimes called the "Fourth World" to distinguish them from "Third World" countries with more hopeful economic prospects — includes some 30 countries with nearly 1 billion people, among them India, Pakistan, Bangladesh, some tropical African countries, and a few countries in Latin America. The World Bank estimates the needs of these countries for additional concessional aid due to the special new factors mentioned above at $0.8 billion in 1974 and $2.1 billion in 1975 — a total of about $3 billion.

The plight of the "Fourth World" countries cannot wait for a general restructuring of the international economic order — a task that may take years. Without emergency measures in the next few months, the shortage of food, energy, and other essential supplies will bring mass starvation, unemployment, and increased hardship for millions already at the economic margin. As Robert S. McNamara, President of the World Bank, put it in his report to the Bank's Executive Board: "Unless substantial additional resources for both long-term investments and immediate balance of payments needs are provided quickly, the hopes of hundreds of millions of people for even modest advances in their economic well-being during the remainder of this decade will be shattered." The result would be a grave weakening of already fragile political and social structures and a clear and present danger of civil violence and even international conflict.

There are two main sources of potential aid for the hard-hit developing countries — the oil producers and the Trilateral world. The oil revenues of the members of the Organization of Petroleum Exporting Countries (OPEC) are expected to increase from about $15 billion in 1972 to about $85 billion in 1974. Those OPEC members with large populations and large development needs (Iran, Algeria, Nigeria, and

Indonesia) will be able to spend all or most of their additional oil revenues on imports. Other OPEC members with relatively sparse populations (Saudi Arabia, Kuwait, Iraq, Libya, Abu Dhabi, and Qatar) will have vast sums available for use overseas.

The countries of the Trilateral region represent the other possible source of help. As a group, they will be paying about $60 billion more for their oil imports in 1974 over 1973. This will both accelerate their rates of inflation — already well into double figures — and aggravate the slowdown in their economies. For most of the Trilateral countries, 1974 will be a year of little growth in real terms — living standards for many of their citizens will actually be lower by the end of 1974 than they were at the beginning. In addition, almost all of the Trilateral countries will suffer large trade deficits as a result of the increased oil costs. However, it should be recalled that the Trilateral countries already stand on a plateau of unprecedented affluence — ranging from an income per capita of over $2,500 in Japan and Europe to over $5,000 in the United States — and that real incomes are expected to rise once again in 1975 and subsequent years after the "oil shock" has been digested and the recession has run its course. Moreover, virtually all of the additional foreign exchange earned by the oil exporting countries will come back to the Trilateral world in the form of new exports or investments. While we do not underestimate the formidable financial adjustments involved, or the difficulties that will face individual countries, we believe they can be managed by the Trilateral world without a general crisis.

Thus the capabilities for a rescue operation on behalf of the hardest hit developing countries are there — the question is the political will to use them. On the one side, the Trilateral countries see their economic prospects diminished, in substantial part because of an oil price increase imposed by the OPEC countries. Some people in the Trilateral countries are saying that the OPEC countries who have profited from the increased oil prices should take the responsibility for helping the developing countries meet the resulting burdens. The OPEC countries, in their turn, point out that the Trilateral countries have reaped gains of their own from price increases of food and fertilizer and industrial goods and reject any suggestion that their oil earnings should be treated differently from earnings on other commodities. They consider the oil price increase as a belated correction for years of unduly cheap oil which benefited the developed countries; and they point out that the combined GNP of the Trilateral world comes to about two trillion dollars, while the combined GNP of the OPEC countries is about $150 billion — less than one-tenth of the Trilateral total.

We must not allow the plight of the non-oil-producing developing countries to worsen while the Trilateral world and the OPEC countries argue about who is to blame for the present crisis. Nor will anything be gained by controversies about what is a "fair" price for oil. In our opinion, the market price for oil during 1950-70 did not adequately reflect its exhaustibility, the need to develop new energy sources, and the general interest in curtailing wasteful consumption. While we also feel that the interests of the oil producing countries as well as of the oil consuming countries would have been better served by a more gradual and somewhat smaller price increase, we believe oil prices may well come down in relative terms over the next few years through changes in energy demand and supply patterns that are now underway. In any event, we feel strongly that a desire to secure a price rollback must not get in the way of urgent measures to help developing countries avoid economic disaster. The financial solutions that will shortly be suggested will have no appreciable effect on the price question. Moreover, it is morally unacceptable to seek an oil price rollback by putting in jeopardy the lives of millions of innocent people.

We believe the proper approach to burden-sharing between the Trilateral world and the OPEC countries is to recognize that the former bear a special responsibility because they have a vastly greater total national income and that the latter also bear a special responsibility because of the dramatic increase in their export earnings and therefore in their capacity to invest sums abroad. To put it another way, the Trilateral countries are wealthy, though not liquid; the OPEC countries are liquid, though not yet wealthy. We therefore propose that an extraordinary act of cooperation be undertaken between the Trilateral and OPEC countries along the following lines:

1.   The two groups of countries should cooperate in making a success of the new "oil facility" proposed by Johannes Witteveen, the Managing Director of the International Monetary Fund. Under this facility, both developed and developing countries facing balance of payments difficulties from increased oil costs will be allowed access to their quotas free from the usual conditions that govern drawings. The Trilateral countries who have substantial amounts of their currencies in the Fund would allow them to be drawn on for this purpose. The OPEC countries with surplus resources would contribute a portion of these to support the oil facility. It is encouraging that some OPEC countries have already made commitments to do this.

2.   To assure the continued flow of development capital to those

developing countries which are able to service loans on near-commercial terms, Trilateral countries that are the beneficiaries of substantial inflows of funds from OPEC countries or whose balance of payments positions are otherwise satisfactory should commit themselves to permit the sale of World Bank bonds in their capital markets, reserving the right to "opt out" of a bond issue only in exceptional cases. In their turn, OPEC countries would undertake to invest a substantial portion of their reserves in these securities.

3. Most importantly, the Trilateral countries and the OPEC countries should make available the $3 billion in extra concessional aid that is needed in 1974-75 for the countries of the "Fourth World."

United Nations Secretary-General Kurt Waldheim, following up a decision of the Special Session of the General Assembly, has issued an appeal to 44 countries to contribute to an emergency program. These 44 countries, by and large, are the countries of the Trilateral and OPEC regions. We believe it is incumbent upon these countries to make prompt and generous contributions.

We believe that the burden of supplying the additional $3 billion in concessional aid should be borne equally by the two groups of countries — the Trilateral world underwriting $1.5 billion, the OPEC countries underwriting the other $1.5 billion. This division of responsibility should be accepted as an ad hoc measure appropriate only to the present emergency and without prejudice to burden-sharing arrangements for the longer term. Aid granted after January 1, 1974 should be counted as a contribution to the emergency program provided it is on concessional terms (grants or long-term credits with very low rates of interest) and provided it is additional to pre-existing aid levels.

The distribution of the aid burden within the two groups of countries would be a matter for negotiation within each group:

We believe the Trilateral countries should share in the $1.5 billion in the same proportion as they are sharing in the $4.5 billion ($1.5 billion per year for three years) called for in the fourth replenishment of the International Development Association. What this would mean in additional commitments by each Trilateral member is indicated in Table 1.* The Trilateral countries would be free to discharge these additional commitments by contributions of additional financial aid or by additional food aid on concessional terms. In exceptional cases where neither of

*For example, the U.S. share of the IDA $4.5 billion is $1.5 billion. Its share of the extra $1.5 billion in concessional aid proposed here would be $500 million.

these forms of assistance is feasible, aid could take the form of postponing debt repayments. The Trilateral countries should also agree to maintain their existing aid flows and make available the sums called for in the agreement on the fourth replenishment of the International Development Association. In this connection favorable action by the U.S. Congress on the pending IDA legislation is needed without further delay.

No already agreed guidelines exist for the apportionment of the other $1.5 billion among the OPEC countries. We note, however, that this sum represents about 2 percent of the $70 billion increase in their oil revenues that took place between 1972 and 1974. Table 2 shows *inter alia* the estimated distribution of oil revenues between OPEC members in 1974 and how each of them has shared in the increase of revenues between 1972 and 1974. Clearly any judgments about burden-sharing to be derived from these figures should take account of the differences in per capita income among the OPEC countries, which is also shown in the Table. Moreover, OPEC countries should have the same flexibility in contributing to the emergency program as the Trilateral countries. They could make their contribution in the form of sales of oil on concessional terms equivalent to U.S. concessional food sales (40 year credits at 3 percent interest) or by increasing bilateral or multilateral financial aid.

We believe the Soviet Union should participate in the $3 billion emergency aid program in the light of its considerable economic capabilities and the fact that it has benefited on the whole from the increase in raw material prices. The spirit of detente and of global solidarity would be importantly strengthened by Soviet cooperation in this initiative to help the "Fourth World." To the extent that the Soviet Union can be persuaded to make a contribution, the amount required from the Trilateral and OPEC countries would be proportionately reduced.

In view of the need for urgent action, time should not be lost in arguments about institutional mechanisms. Assistance can be given through bilateral arrangements, institutions of the OPEC countries, or existing multilateral institutions such as the International Bank/International Development Association, the Regional Development Banks, and the World Food Program. The important thing is that the assistance be made available quickly and in sufficient amounts. However, it should be emphasized that assistance should take the form of program aid and not be tied to specific projects. Moreover, it will be necessary for some central institution to certify that contributions are made in an appropriate form and are received by countries in the category of those requiring extra concessional aid.

While we recommend flexibility on institutional forms in the interest of launching the emergency program, we do favor the use wherever possible of existing multilateral institutions. They possess a fund of experience and a reservoir of technical and managerial skill that is not easily duplicated.

There are a number of options open to the OPEC and Trilateral countries that could make use of these existing institutions while assuring the donors of a satisfactory measure of control over the use of their funds:

— use of the multilateral institutions as executing agencies for bilateral or regional aid programs approved by Trilateral or OPEC countries;

— case-by-case participation by Trilateral or OPEC countries in loans of the multilateral institutions (as in the recent IBRD loan to Syria, half of which was subscribed by the Kuwait fund);

— creation of a "special fund" for OPEC contributions in the IBRD/IDA with special voting and decision-making arrangements governing use of that fund;

— direct contributions to the concessional funds of these institutions, with appropriate renegotiation in voting rights and decision-making arrangements.

If it should prove impossible to use the latter two approaches in time for the emergency program, they should certainly be explored for the longer run. In this connection, we note the estimate of the World Bank that in the period 1976-80 the developing countries will require $4 to $5 billion a year of extra concessional aid in order to meet their minimum development goals. This additional requirement will result not only from the increased cost of imports but from the running down of the developing countries' monetary reserves and the expected deterioration in their terms of trade associated with the slowing down in the growth rate of the developed countries. It is not too soon to begin exploring how multilateral institutions might be adapted to facilitate Trilateral-OPEC cooperation in development beyond the emergency program. Nor is it too soon to examine how, through the development of indigenous food and energy resources, the curbing of excessive population growth, and other measures to be mentioned later, the economic and social goals of developing countries can be realized in the 1980's without indefinite infusions of large amounts of concessional aid.

We believe the time has also come for high-level negotiations between Trilateral and OPEC countries aimed at assisting the latter in the diversification and development of their own economies. The leaders of the oil exporting nations are understandably concerned that measures be taken now to assure a sound economic future for their people after their petroleum resources are depleted. To the extent that the Trilateral countries assist in the solution of this problem, Trilateral-OPEC cooperation in short and longer-term measures to help the non-oil-producing developing countries is likely to be enhanced. One obvious area of mutual interest which needs to be explored is the establishment of fertilizer production in the OPEC countries of the Middle East, combining the abundant oil and gas of these countries with capital and technology from the industrial world. The output of such facilities could be used not only in the area but also in the fertilizer-short countries of the Indian subcontinent.

In our opinion, time is now of the essence. The full impact of the plight of the developing countries has not registered so far because financial settlements for oil are made quarterly and bills for oil shipped at the new high prices are only just coming due. The "crunch" will come this summer when accounts for the second quarter of the year have to be settled. We call on the Trilateral countries, in their enlightened self-interest, to assume shared responsibility with the members of OPEC in this new venture of cooperation to cope with the present emergency before it is too late.

II

Even as the Trilateral countries respond to the present emergency, they must begin the longer-term task of helping to build a new and more satisfactory international economic order. Our work thus far, aided by consultations with experts from both developed and developing countries, has led us to the following broad conclusions about the new approaches that need to be developed for North-South economic relations:

1. Both developed and developing countries need to give greater weight in policy-making to their growing interdependence. For the Trilateral region, this means that liberal aid and trade measures on behalf of developing countries should be undertaken not only because "it is right" but because the Trilateral world increasingly needs the developing countries as sources of raw materials, as export markets, and most important of all, as constructive partners in the operation of a workable world political and economic order. In the months and years ahead, the Trilateral countries will be engaged in negotiations with

developing countries on a broad range of issues including finance and trade, energy and resources, and the law of the sea. Slowly but surely, a new system of relationships is being negotiated in place of the old one that emerged from the postwar era. This new system will not emerge unless it adequately reflects the views and interests of the developing countries; it will not survive unless these countries feel they have a stake in it.

2. The new system of relationships must respect the right to independence and equality under international law of all members of the world community, rich and poor, large and small. We categorically reject not only old-fashioned colonialism but also latter-day concepts of neo-colonialism, paternalism and tutelage. All countries should be free to determine their own political, economic and social systems, free of external coercion. At the same time, any system of full equality must acknowledge that every member of the community has obligations as well as rights. The obligation of wealthy countries to provide assistance is matched by an obligation of developing countries to use assistance to improve the quality of life for the masses and not just for a privileged few. Development is mainly the result of local effort; thus developed countries have a legitimate interest in the progress made by developing countries in mobilizing the energies of their people through reforms in their political, economic and social structures. The way for developed countries to express this legitimate interest is through cooperative programs with developing countries in which changes in domestic policies are sought through a process of mutual persuasion, and not imposed by outside dictation. Foreign investment is a particularly sensitive area where the rights and obligations of developed and developing countries need to be carefully balanced. Developing countries should be free to determine whether and under what conditions they wish to accept foreign investment. Yet all countries bear the obligation of fair treatment for foreigners and their property — a concept that applies both to developing countries' citizens and investments in developed countries and vice-versa. The practical application of this principle must find an appropriate balance between respect for contract and property rights, on the one hand, and the need to assure mutuality of benefits on the other, and there may be circumstances in which arrangements originating in a period of unequal bargaining power will need to be revised.

3. There is no room in such a new system of relationships for the concept of "spheres of influence" or even "spheres of responsibility." We reject the idea that special aid and trade policies should be developed tying Africa to Europe, Latin America to the United States or Southeast

Asia to Japan. This does not exclude the free collaboration between developed and developing countries of the same region on projects based on mutual economic interest. What it does rule out are the exchange of tariff preferences between limited groups of developed and developing countries or the granting of military and economic aid in return for preferred access to raw materials. We must avoid the temptation that faces the Trilateral countries in a period of resource scarcity to concentrate their aid and trade favors on a relatively few resource-rich developing countries while ignoring the needs of the rest. A system that emphasizes multilateral aid flows and multilateral trade concessions is most likely to prevent this development and serve the long-term interests of all.

4. The policies of both governments and international organizations should reflect greater recognition of the differing needs and capabilities of different developing countries. From an economic point of view, the so-called "Third World" has become at least three worlds — the oil producing countries earning huge amounts of foreign exchange, the relatively well-off developing countries with other valuable resources or a growing industrial base, and the "have-not" developing countries such as those in the Indian subcontinent and the Sahelian zone of Africa. Emphasis on these differences is not motivated by a desire to break up the unity of the developing world — the developing countries will continue to unite when they have common interests — it is motivated rather by a desire to adapt policies to new realities so that the legitimate interests of all will be served. For example, concessional aid should henceforth be concentrated on the have-not developing countries that need it most, with other developing countries making contributions of capital and technical assistance in accordance with their emerging capabilities.

5. The interests of both developed and developing countries will be better served in this historical period by cooperation than by confrontation. We recognize that this statement has a hollow ring in the light of the failure of developed countries to live up to the aid and trade targets of the two U.N. Development Decades. It is true that confrontation sometimes brings short-term benefits. But in the longer-run — particularly in the difficult economic and political conditions of the mid-1970's — it is bound to stimulate defensive and harmful responses from the governments and peoples of the developed world. The developed countries who have the military, political and economic power can only be persuaded by appeals to mutual interest; emphasis on adversary interests and the abuse of automatic majorities in international agencies

is likely to delay the desired adjustments. At the same time, the developed countries must realize that confrontation has resulted from past failures of cooperation for which they bear a heavy responsibility and that more responsive policies will be required on their part if cooperation is to be possible in the future.

6. Much more must be done to assure that development efforts help the bottom 40 percent of the population in the developing countries. Donor and recipient countries, working together in their mutual interest, should promote development programs that stress not only increases in GNP but also the "qualitative" aspects of development — the eradication of extreme poverty, a better distribution of income and wealth, the improvement of rural welfare, the reduction of unemployment, and broad access to education, health and social services. Two key elements in such a "people-oriented" development strategy should be measures to increase the productivity of the small farmer and to adapt technologies to situations where labor is abundant and capital scarce. Another key element is effective action to reduce population growth, which in many developing countries threatens to overwhelm efforts to improve the quality of life. We believe that all countries should adopt and implement realistic population policies as an integral part of their development plans.

7. New rules and arrangements governing access to supplies should be part of a new system of relations between developed and developing countries. Such new rules and arrangements would be in the general interest, for at least four reasons: First, developing countries as a group are as dependent on developed countries for supplies of food and manufactured goods as developed countries are dependent on them for supplies of energy and raw materials. The logic of interdependence suggests the need for some agreed limits on the ability of producers to cut off the essential supplies of others for political or economic reasons. Second, countries faced with the prospect of supply cut-offs are likely to seek more secure alternatives through policies of national or regional self-sufficiency — thus export controls breed import controls. Third, the availability of substitutes and synthetics and lower grade ores sets serious limits on the practicability of producer cartels for commodities other than oil; thus while such cartels may occasionally yield short-term results to the participants they are likely to be self-defeating in the longer run. Fourth, the "have-not" developing countries have the greatest stake in reasonable access to food, energy and other supplies. Any international system that leaves them at the mercy of supplying countries fails to meet minimum requirements of economic justice. Having said all this, we

recognize that access to supplies is not likely to be negotiated except in the context of a more satisfactory international system. The challenge to developed and developing countries is to fashion a "world order bargain" in which access to supplies is traded for other kinds of access — access to markets at stable and remunerative prices, access to technology and capital, and access to a reasonable share of decision-making in international economic forums.

We realize only too well that the broad concepts outlined above are much easier to define than implement successfully. Such concepts will become really meaningful only as developed and developing countries find answers to such questions as the following:

— How can political support be created in the Trilateral countries for liberal aid and trade policies at a time of acute inflation, stagnant growth, rising unemployment and political instability?

— What specific changes in the policies of governments and international agencies would be necessary to implement a "people-oriented" aid strategy?

— Is it in the interest of the Trilateral countries to support the establishment of substantial new sources of development assistance independent of annual government decision-making, such as the "link" with SDR creation or revenues from seabed exploitation?

— How can the Trilateral countries open their markets to the agricultural and manufactured exports of the developing countries while assuring orderly internal adjustment?

— How can the potential of foreign investment in general and the multinational corporation in particular be utilized consistently with the needs and aspirations of developing countries?

— What specific rules on supply access would be desirable and feasible as part of the "world order bargain"?

— What kind of commodity agreements — and for which specific commodities — would serve the interest of both exporting and importing countries?

— In particular, what kind of cooperative arrangements and joint ventures would harmonize the oil exporting countries' interests in industrialization and diversification with the oil importing countries' needs for secure and reasonably priced energy supplies?

The answers to these questions will not be quickly or easily found. But the prospects for finding solutions would be enhanced by the right kind of institutional framework. We therefore propose to devote our second report to the restructuring of the international institutions governing North-South economic relations.

It is no secret that the existing institutional system is the subject of widespread criticism from both developed and developing countries. Questions have been raised about the "politicalization" of economic discussions, about methods of creating, changing, interpreting and enforcing the rules, about the efficiency and impartiality of the international civil service, and about the difficulty of coordinating the growing number of functional and regional structures.

Perhaps most important of all, there is a growing dissatisfaction with voting and decision-making arrangements. It is already clear to us that the developing countries, and particularly the oil producing countries, should have more voting rights and a greater role in the management of the International Monetary Fund and World Bank group. At the same time, some procedural reforms are needed in those forums such as the General Assembly, UNCTAD and GATT where the one-nation one-vote principle fails to reflect fairly the balance of economic interest and power. Differential voting rights may be difficult to negotiate, but resort can also be had to special majority requirements, committees with selective representation, and conciliation procedures using impartial and expert third parties. Obviously institutional changes cannot be a substitute for political will, but such reforms could help promote a sense of confidence in the objectivity and effectiveness of international institutions that is presently lacking.

In the preparation of this report, we have come to see a close relation between our proposals for emergency action and these longer-term questions of institutional restructuring. Without effective action to deal with the urgent plight of the hardest-hit developing countries, the prospects of creating a new and better relationship between the Trilateral world and the developing world will be dim indeed. Yet unless we keep in mind some vision of the new international economic order we want to create, it is unlikely that we will find satisfactory answers to the immediate crisis. It is our hope that by identifying both the short and longer-term issues in North-South relations we may hasten the day when interdependence becomes not just a convenient slogan but a working system.

TABLE 1
COMPARATIVE INDICATORS FOR IDA CONTRIBUTING COUNTRIES

(figures in the first column should be divided by 3 to give the indicated additional contribution in emergency aid.)

Contributing Countries	Fourth Replenishment Contribution (millions U.S. dollars equivalent and percentage of total)		Third Replenishment Contribution (millions U.S. dollars equivalent and percentage of total)		% of Combined GNP of Contributing Countries	Official Development Assistance as % GNP in 1972	Population (millions)
Part I Countries							
Australia	$ 90.0	2.0%	$ 48.0	2.0%	1.72%	.61%	12.3
Austria	30.6	0.7	16.3	0.7	.77	.09	7.4
Belgium	76.5	1.7	40.8	1.7	1.34	.55	9.6
Canada	274.5	6.1	150.0	6.1	3.93	.47	21.1
Denmark	54.0	1.2	26.4	1.1	.78	.45	4.9
Finland	25.2	0.5	12.2	0.5	.49	(a)	4.7
France	253.5	5.6	150.0	6.1	7.51	.67	50.3
Germany	514.5	11.4	234.0	9.6	9.77	.31	60.8
Iceland	1.3	0.03	—	—	.03	(a)	(b)
Ireland	7.5	0.2	3.9	0.2	.20	(a)	2.7
Italy	181.3	4.0	96.7	4.0	4.37	.09	53.2
Japan	495.0	11.0	144.0	5.9	11.27	.21	102.3
Kuwait	27.0	0.6	10.8	0.4	.13	(a)	0.6
Luxembourg	2.2	.05	1.2	.05	.05	(a)	0.3
Netherlands	132.7	2.9	67.5	2.8	1.71	.67	12.9
New Zealand	11.7	0.26	3.3	0.25(c)	.31	(a)	2.8
Norway	49.5	1.1	24.0	1.0	.58	.41	3.9
South Africa	9.0	0.2	3.0	0.1	.72	(a)	20.2
Sweden	180.0	4.0	102.0	4.2	1.52	.48	8.0
United Kingdom	499.5	11.1	311.0	12.7	5.75	.40	55.5
United States	1,500.0	33.3	960.0	40.0	43.36	.29	203.2
Part II Countries							
Israel	1.0	.02	—	—	.26	(a)	2.9
Spain	13.3	.30	2.5	0.1	1.73	(a)	22.5
Yugoslavia	5.0	.11	4.0	0.2	.58	(a)	20.5
Switzerland (NOT MEMBER OF IDA)	66.1	1.50	30.0	1.2	1.14	.21	6.2
Totals	$4,500.0	100.0	$2,442.0	100.0	100.0		

(a) Not members of the Development Assistance Committee (DAC)   (b) Less than one million   (c) Not member of IDA for Third Replenishment

(a) Not member of IDA

73

TABLE 2

Estimated Oil Revenues, Per Capita GNP, Population, and Total Imports of Eleven OPEC Countries

Country	Estimated Government Oil Revenue ($ millions)			Estimated Per Capita Government Oil Revenue $			Per Capita GNP $	Population (millions)	Total Imports ($ millions)	
	1972	1973	1974	1972	1973	1974a)	1971	1973	1971	1972
Saudi Arabia	2,988	4,915	19,400	393	630	2,456	540	7.8	806	1,229
Iran	2,423	3,885	14,930	79	123	461	450	31.5	1,871	2,410
Kuwait	1,600	2,130	7,945	1,758	2,131	7,223	3,860	1.0	678	797
Iraq	802	1,465	5,900	80	141	551	370	10.4	696	713
Abu Dhabi	538	1,035	4,800	11,700	22,565	43,636	3,150	0.1	n.a.	n.a.
Qatar	247	360	1,425	1,941	2,575	9,500	2,370	0.1	n.a.	n.a.
Venezuela	1,933	2,800	10,010	176	250	870	1,060	11.2	2,301	2,433
Libya	1,705	2,210	7,990	820	1,005	3,631	1,450	2.2	712	1,101
Nigeria	1,200	1,950	6,960	21	33	114	140	59.4	1,506	1,502
Algeria	680	1,095	3,700	45	71	233	360	15.4	1,221	1,760
Indonesia	480	830	2,150	4	7	17	80	124.0	1,174	1,458

a) ODC estimate based on World Bank estimates for OPEC government oil revenues, population (mid-1971), and population growth rates.

SOURCES: Oil revenue figures are informal World Bank staff estimates. GNP and population figures are from *World Bank Atlas, 1974* (Washington, D.C.: World Bank Group, 1974). Import figures are based on *International Trade, 1972* (Geneva: General Agreement on Tariffs and Trade, 1973), Publication Sales No. GATT 1973-3.

DIRECTIONS FOR WORLD TRADE

IN THE NINETEEN-SEVENTIES

Guido Colonna di Paliano
*Former Member of the
European Community
Commission*

Philip H. Trezise
*Senior Fellow,
The Brookings
Institution*

Nobuhiko Ushiba
*Former Ambassador
of Japan to
the United States*

Table of Contents

I. WHY A TRADE NEGOTIATION

At Tokyo last September more than 100 sovereign nations agreed to undertake a new multilateral negotiation on the conditions governing world trade. This will be the seventh negotiation to be held under the aegis of that useful and durable international contract, the General Agreement on Tariffs and Trade. It has the promise of being the most comprehensive yet. It may also prove to be the most important, in a sense larger than its trade aspects alone, for it will offer an opportunity to restore and strengthen an international structure of cooperation that has been weakened by time and by neglect.

To some, to be sure, the timing of this renewed international effort to improve the trading system is wildly inauspicious. There is a palpable air of uncertainty about the world economy. Most countries face unprecedented payments problems deriving from the sharp rise in oil prices. Shortages, of commodities and of processing capacity, have been general, and some are likely to persist even as world economic activity slows down. Worries about the adequacy of food supplies, in the short and long run, have not been laid to rest. Inflation has become a global phenomenon. The monetary system is in disarray, at least if we think of a system as operating under agreed rules. One of the pillars of the European Community — the customs union — seemingly has been put in jeopardy. In these circumstances, it may be asked, is it prudent to begin a major multilateral negotiation in the course of which the parties will be expected to make new commitments to reduce and remove their protective trade barriers?

The answer, it seems to us, is that the multilateral negotiation decided upon at Tokyo is precisely relevant to many, although of course not all, of the world's current economic difficulties. Trade policy is one of the keys to a more efficient use of limited resources. It thus bears directly on the problem of shortages. Even though we obviously cannot claim that the GATT negotiation can eliminate immediate inflationary pressures, it will be addressed to the enduring problem of scarcity and thereby real costs and prices.

Looking at specific problems, it is clear that if we are to have greater protection against supply disruptions, we must have a multilateral structure of supply assurances and stronger guidelines on how export restrictions may be applied, if at all. Non-tariff trade distorting measures probably have become more damaging to trade in recent years; this trend can be arrested only by negotiations to tighten the rules and to develop new ones. Tensions in the trade relations between the advanced industrial countries and the developing world have worsened under the debate-confrontation procedure that has been so much in vogue; substantive negotiations afford the possibility of relieving these tensions.

We have also considered the argument that another GATT trade round is an attempt to apply the techniques of the past to a world that has changed in radical ways. This misses the point, we think. It is certainly true that some of the preoccupying issues of the moment are novel, or relatively so; export restrictions, for instance, have only incidentally been considered during past trade negotiations. But the objective should be exactly to find multilateral understandings and procedures to deal with these new issues. That earlier negotiations have been more narrowly confined in no way precludes or proscribes innovation in this round. Indeed, as we develop in subsequent pages, nearly all of the subjects that would make up a comprehensive negotiating agenda would have little precedent in GATT experience. A serious negotiation inevitably will have to break a vast amount of new ground.

One of the matters in debate prior to the Tokyo meeting was whether a trade negotiation could proceed without a restoration of order in the monetary field. The Tokyo Declaration sensibly recognizes that trade and monetary problems must be considered concurrently. The links between them argue for progress on both, not for priority for one or the other.

It should be clear, however, that the trade and monetary negotiations do deal with different aspects of the international economy. A monetary system, if it works well, is a mechanism for facilitating trade, investment, and tourism *in general* and for enabling across-the-board adjustments to be made when *general* shifts in underlying economic conditions occur. Thus a change in a country's exchange rate affects all its prices in the international market, both for imports and for exports, and for all its other foreign transactions as well. We need a system that assures that such changes will work toward general equilibrium, that is that they respond to basic market forces rather than to manipulation for special advantage.

Trade measures typically are particular in their effects. Protection is normally afforded to some products, not to all. Even a generalized trade action — a surcharge on all imports, say — can only be partial and thereby distorting in its impact. The aim of a trade negotiation is to reduce and minimize these particular distortions and the costs that go with them, leaving it to the monetary system to correct general disequilibria. And, as is noted in the Tokyo Declaration, liberalized trade will facilitate the orderly functioning of the monetary system, just as it is true that a well-working monetary system will promote trade.

In brief, we believe that the reasons that have been arrayed against having another trade negotiation lack merit. We think that there is no good alternative, that the case for going ahead is overriding. Autarchic or bilateral solutions to the problems of the day hold out no real promise. Special bilateral deals for oil cannot give insurance against high prices or, in the end, against arbitrary interruptions of supplies. Commodity shortages have contributed to the frightening phenomenon of global inflation but few if any nations can improve their price performances in the short or the long run by opting for greater domestic self-sufficiency. Attempts to cope with the secondary effects of the escalation of oil prices on an individual country basis — say, by restrictionist import policies and the artificial promotion of exports — is sure to lead to frustration and quite possibly to disastrously costly commercial hostilities among the chief trading countries. The shortcomings or failures of the existing multilateral economic institutions certainly cannot be remedied by a drift to national or regional insulation from world economic affairs.

If the world was now to shelve the Tokyo agreement to negotiate, the result would be a further period of marking time in which the erosion of the multilateral arrangements that have supported the long postwar prosperity would continue unchecked. There is more here than questions of narrow economic advantage or disadvantage. The world, but particularly the principal industrial regions, has a fundamental political stake in the strengthening of rules and obligations, and institutional devices, through which national economic interests can be guarded by setting tolerable restraints on unilateral national actions. No one can foresee now the results of the large and complex negotiation that is still in its early stages. The goal is nevertheless clear. It is to make economic interdependence, which is inescapable in the modern world, a more manageable and less troubling condition. Or, what is the same thing, it is to find a range of livable compromises between the legitimate claims of national sovereignty and the imperatives of international order.

II.   The Negotiating Issues

It seems certain that the scope of a new trade negotiation will be wider than any in the past. Six rounds of general trade negotiations took place between 1947 and 1967, of which only the first (when the GATT was agreed upon) and last ventured beyond tariffs as such. These negotiations, and the provisions of the GATT itself, achieved significant reductions in preexisting obstacles to trade. Industrial tariffs were brought down *on the average* to quite modest levels, quota restrictions were banned in principle, and a range of other trade-limiting or trade-distorting measures were subjected to international rule. But one whole trading sector, agriculture, came to be treated so exceptionally as to be put largely outside the system. For a number of reasons, to be discussed in a later section, the GATT's effectiveness in the consistent application of its provisions was far from perfect. And, as was inevitable, changes in the GATT have lagged behind changes in world trade patterns and practices.

The seventh GATT round, as foreshadowed by the Tokyo Declaration, therefore has within its aegis the old issues — including those ignored in the past — and some new issues as well. They may be listed as follows:

- Tariffs on industrial goods, the standby of past GATT rounds
- The conditions of agricultural trade
- Non-tariff measures
- Export controls and scarce supplies
- Safeguards against import disruption
- Reform of the GATT
- Trade relations with the third world

Before turning to an examination of each of these, we may observe that we have consciously limited the scope of our discussion to them. Other subjects readily could be included within the range of trade policies of substantial trilateral concern. They include the special problems relating to trade with the USSR and Communist China, the questions surrounding direct foreign investment and the role of the multinational corporation, and particular features of trade in energy resources. These are separable topics, however, and we believe they should be treated apart both to do them full justice and to avoid an unduly extended report here.

III.   Do Tariffs Still Matter?

The short answer is that tariffs do matter. They remain the most pervasive restraint on international trade. While a negotiation strictly limited to tariffs on industrial goods would be doomed, a round that failed to focus on industrial tariffs would also fail.

Despite six rounds of postwar reductions, tariffs continue to be applied to 60 percent of international trade in industrial goods. The average dutiable rate of 10 percent masks many higher duties, some of them prohibitive in their effect. Beyond that, the proper measure of a tariff's impact on industrial trade is not its *nominal* level but rather the *effective* rate on the value added by manufacture. Effective rates are very often considerably higher than the listed tariffs. In practice, also, the most onerous duties and the highest effective rates tend to be applicable to labor-intensive goods, which contrasts wryly with the many verbal commitments to greater market access for the exports of the developing countries. Finally, of course, even quite low tariff rates can sway investment decisions and lead to misallocations of resources.

It is inconceivable, in any case, that the occasion of a major trade negotiation would not be taken to try to reduce the commercially discriminatory and the politically divisive impact of the Western European free trade area, which seems bound to emerge from the arrangements between the Community and the former European Free Trade Association (EFTA) nations. The United States, Canada, Japan, Australia, and others will wish to negotiate reductions of Community tariffs and those of the other Western European states so as to mitigate growing Europe-wide discrimination against their exports. This will have to be a reciprocal process. The bargaining will not be easy, for the Community's external tariff is not only protective of affected industries but is symbolic of European integration. Nonetheless, a bargained reduction of tariffs offers the only practicable answer to the free trade area problem, which cannot be wished away. As for the Community's special preferential arrangements with other countries, they are much less important commercially. But here too a general cut in duties would help to relieve fears of an impending division of the trading world into rival blocs.

Most economists today would argue for a progressive, across-the-board, and automatic reduction and elimination of tariffs on industrial products. This approach would promise a maximum of results and it would greatly simplify the negotiating procedure. The success of the EC and the EFTA in cutting tariffs by an automatic formula suggests that it would be practical to do so on a wider scale. In fact, the "working hypothesis" advanced by the United States and Japan in 1972 at the GATT was essentially for an automatic, phased elimination of duties.

The EC, however, has made clear that it is not prepared to consider eliminating its tariffs at this time, and the American government apparently will not be given the requisite authority to do so by the Congress. Thus it will be necessary to find an alternative approach to tariff bargaining. The broad goal surely should be maximum tariff reductions, staged over a transitional period that is long enough to allow affected industries time to adjust to new competitive situations; it is useful to recall that both the EC and the EFTA found it possible to eliminate their internal tariffs in fewer than ten years. How to negotiate the particulars is less evident, however.

Among possible negotiating techniques, three are commonly advanced:

— A linear reduction of tariffs in stages by an agreed standard percentage. This was the basic Kennedy Round principle, although in practice it had to be qualified by numerous exceptions and modifications.

— Tariff harmonization which in its strictest form would mean the same tariff levels everywhere for similar goods, but which can also be taken to mean a levelling down of high tariffs without aiming for identical rates. It has long been a European Community position that the disparately high tariffs in American, Canadian, and Japanese schedules should be scaled down more nearly toward the comparatively level ranges of EC duties. The Kennedy Round negotiations dealt with the tariff disparities question, but on a limited scale and only after long and hard bargaining over the thorny problem of reciprocity.

— Sector-by-sector negotiations, which strictly read might call for separate reciprocal bargains industry-by-industry. In that form, the approach holds out minimum hope for results. Apart from the difficulties about defining industrial sectors, the problem of satisfying the claims to reciprocity by this method is all but insoluble. Still, the problems of particular industries are certain to enter the negotiation and some measure of intra-sectoral bargaining cannot be foreclosed.

The pending American legislation would allow the U.S. negotiators to offer (a) to eliminate tariffs of five percent ad valorem or less; (b) to reduce by 60 percent tariffs between five and twenty-five percent; and (c) to reduce by 75 percent tariffs above twenty-five percent, provided that the new duties must not fall below ten percent. If these are the eventual American negotiating ranges they will set the outer limits of the international tariff bargaining, since the Congress is not likely to enlarge its grant of authority once the negotiations are under way.

As a practical matter, the American formula affords a considerable degree of negotiating flexibility. Under its terms it should be possible to devise a working hypothesis or general rule for reducing duties which would accommodate to a degree pressures for reductions in the disparately high tariffs (possibly by setting average upper limits of broad industrial categories). Sensitive industrial sectors undoubtedly will have to be given special attention, but the commitment to a general rule will help to keep this problem within bounds.

IV. The Elements of an Agricultural Bargain

As the odd man out of postwar liberalization, agricultural trade has been the source of chronic quarrels among the principal members of the GATT. The blame can be assigned widely and impartially. It was the United States that insisted in 1955, to much dismay elsewhere, upon a waiver that entirely freed its agriculture from the restraints of the GATT. Most of the other contracting parties chose for their part to protect their vulnerable farm products without bothering with the waiver process. The European Community's common agricultural policy (CAP) turned out to be a program not only for insulating its agriculture from world markets but also for promoting large surpluses to be off-loaded abroad with the aid of export subsidies. In the Kennedy Round, agricultural trade was the object of a prolonged, bitter, partly theological exchange, ending with the hastily contrived International Grains Arrangement, which collapsed within a few months.

We consider that in another negotiation a fresh start should be made on the conditions of international trade in agriculture, in the first instance among the industrial countries which account normally for most of the commercial trade in farm commodities.

To begin, current prices of the chief traded farm commodities are high enough so that trade flows are largely unimpeded by the national or regional restrictions designed specifically to protect domestic prices. It is a period, therefore, in which some of the earlier international tensions have diminished and in which a calmer view of the changing agricultural scene should be possible. Second, the vulnerabilities in the present structure of world agriculture have been dramatically shown, in the aftermath of the USSR's exceptionally bad 1972 harvest. The need to reexamine agricultural trade relations can hardly be ignored.

If, of course, present inflated levels of world agricultural prices are expected to remain unchanged indefinitely, the exporting countries might see a negotiation as being irrelevant in that trade barriers would have become ineffective. In that case, the import needs of a number of developing countries, most importantly in South Asia, would present continuing and acute problems. These would not be manageable on a commercial basis, obviously, and would call for a food aid effort that would be extremely difficult to mount.

The likely outlook, however, is not for unchanged high prices. It is commonly overlooked that wheat acreage in the United States, Canada, and Australia had been deliberately cut back after 1968 in order, as the United Nations Food and Agriculture Organization put it, to cope with "production in excess of available outlets." The USSR's crop failure in 1972 thus came when the world's chief exporters were restricting output and when stocks, except for those in the United States, had already been depleted. With a relaxation of acreage restrictions in 1973, wheat production in the three exporting countries went up by 20 percent. And while world demand will continue to rise, as population and incomes rise, so will farm productivity. So the prudent guess must be that we shall see during the next few years a return to agricultural relationships in which output in the exporting nations will tend to outrun effective demand in most years, and the old questions of protectionism and dumping will again be before us. At the same time, however, the recent experience of short supplies and export controls will keep in the picture the question of security of supplies.

These two considerations — potential surpluses and worries about supplies — suggest the essential elements of a bargain. On the one hand, the more efficient agricultural producers will have a claim to improved conditions of market access, whether for cereals or dairy products. On the other, importing nations properly can ask for assurances that their normal requirements will be met in all predictable circumstances.

During the Kennedy Round the discussions centered briefly on a Community concept that was given the label *montant de soutien,* or level of support. It was not fully explored then, but the basic idea offers the most promising approach to the access problem, which derives mainly from efforts to protect domestic support levels from import competition. In effect, the procedure would be to determine, first, the difference between an agreed world base price for each of the commodities concerned and the intervention or target level in the importing country or region. These differences or margins of protection would then be frozen and thereafter gradually reduced. Both steps would have to be negotiated. There is no automatic formula here. Political realities doubtless would require a limit on the possible reductions in protection in any year or over any stated period. Allowance would have to be made for rising price levels. Exceptional treatment would have to be given to programs applied specifically to low income farmers and disadvantaged regions.

Security of supply must in the end rest upon the physical availability of stocks. Long-term purchase contracts may give reasonable assurance to one or a few importing nations, but not to all. Once a sufficiently bad harvest has occurred, only reserves in being can make up the resulting shortage.

In the past, the United States and Canada alone have held agricultural stocks and then principally in order to support domestic price levels. An international program would set out deliberately to build stocks, presumably mainly of cereals but possibly also of oilseeds and some other commodities, on the basis of shared responsibilities. The costs of acquiring and holding the stocks would be borne by individual governments, with their target levels determined according to volumes of production or consumption, or a combination of the two. Releases from stockpiles could be according to mutual agreement under predetermined guidelines, or the criterion could be price. Buffer stock operations to iron out year-to-year price fluctuations could be fitted into the general stockpiling agreement; these would involve commitments to add to stocks when output rose above trend and to sell when crops fell short of the average.

In our opinion, agriculture is sufficiently special a case as to require a substantially self-contained negotiation within the general round. The notion that industrial concessions can be traded for agricultural concessions has little support in experience or in the nature of the trade problem. The eventual result should be a balanced agricultural settlement, covering security of supply and reductions of import protection, whatever the actual protective techniques may be. What will be necessary is a readiness by all those participating to be prepared to offer modifications in their own restrictions on imports. The United States and Canada, for instance, could hardly expect to reach a package agreement involving the Community that did not offer improved conditions of access for European dairy products into North American markets.

A separate settlement for agriculture also would have to deal with some of the main non-tariff measures. An access-stockpile agreement would bring the issue of export subsidies for the major crops under closer control by reducing incentives to produce surpluses by providing for the disposition of excess output in stocks. This might be supplemented by a general commitment to place the use of subsidies under agreed rules and to make them subject to mandatory consultation with competing suppliers. The other principal kind of non-tariff measure in agriculture is the quota restriction, which is applied to a wide range of farm products. Quotas are illegal *per se* under the GATT, but on agricultural goods (as is true of coal) they have sanction of long usage and their wholesale elimination is not a reasonable possibility. But an obligation to increase quota levels annually, subject to minimum exceptions, might be an acceptable compromise within an overall agricultural bargain.

We stress that we have only sketched the outlines of a possible agricultural agreement. Its negotiation would be perhaps the most difficult task of all those on the international agenda. If something like it could be arrived at, there would have to be a far reaching extension of international cooperative effort. The agreement could not be self-executing. It would require exchanges of information, consultation, and joint decision-making on a significant scale. Non-participating industrial countries — the USSR of course being the most important — inescapably would be drawn into consultation about its implications and perhaps into membership.

In this section we have discussed an agricultural trade negotiation between the industrial countries, with the United States, Canada, Australia, Japan, and the Community as the principal parties. The compelling agricultural and food needs of the developing nations of course must be considered in any review of the conditions of agricultural trade. We shall therefore come back to the subject when we turn to the trade problems of the less developed world.

V. Non-Tariff Distortions of Trade

The Tokyo Declaration contains a commitment to "reduce or eliminate non-tariff measures or, where this is not appropriate, to reduce or eliminate their trade restricting or distorting effects, and to bring such measures under more effective international discipline."

This carefully phrased passage reflects the range and the complexity of the non-tariff issue. Only a few of the non-tariff measures will lend themselves to quick and decisive disposition. Some will require agreement on definitions and interpretations before procedures can be established for dealing with them. Reciprocal bargains of the kind customary in tariff negotiations may be possible on a few matters, but mostly the search will be for codes of conduct to be applied by the contracting parties. The non-tariff field is preeminently one for a strengthening and tightening of international rules, rather than for definitive trade-offs.

Any categorization of the many practices lumped under the term non-tariff measures must be arbitrary. The following list is probably fairly inclusive, however:

— Quantitative controls on imports and, now, on exports
— Burdensome customs and administrative entry procedures
— Subsidies to exports and the defensive measures taken against them, e.g. anti-dumping and countervailing duty policies
— Industrial, safety, health, or environmental standards applied discriminatorily against imports
— Discriminatory public procurement policies
— Government aids to industry which have protective effects

If, as we suggest should be done, the agricultural negotiation was to be handled as a substantially separate package, some of these categories — import quotas and export subsidies and limitations on exports — would be reduced in their scope. There will still remain, nevertheless, a very wide area for fact-finding, rule-making, and negotiation.

Fortunately, the GATT parties and its Secretariat began immediately after the end of the Kennedy Round in 1967 to assemble data and to consider strategies for acting on non-tariff measures. General guidelines have been drafted for the application of industrial and other standards. Progress has been made toward more precise definitions of customs valuation practices covered by Article 7 of the General Agreement. The OECD has spent more than a decade in an as yet fruitless effort to arrive at a convention on public purchasing; the problems and alternatives have been minutely studied. In other cases a good deal of preliminary work has been done.

Building on what has been done thus far, including the limited and ultimately abortive non-tariff bargains struck during the Kennedy Round, a negotiation could accomplish a significant improvement in the conditions of international trade. The non-tariff articles scattered through the GATT could be made subject to interpretive notes. International codes could be drawn for such matters as public procurement policies and the operation of national or regional standards. A relatively small number of non-tariff distortions — import quotas on industrial products and the American Selling Price customs valuation rule in the United States are examples — might be eliminated outright, either in special bargains or as a part of a general dismantling of trade barriers. Even in so sensitive an area as government aids to industry, it should be possible to design a set of principles that would distinguish between, say, regional development incentives of a preponderantly protective character and those which may be construed as primarily offsetting of actual local disabilities.

An important question is whether any extension of GATT obligations in the non-tariff field should be subject to the basic GATT rule of unconditional most-favored-nation treatment. In some instances — customs valuation procedures for example — anything else would probably be impracticable. But should the parties to a code governing public procurement apply the rule of non-discrimination to countries that are unwilling to accept the code? We think that the European Community's view here is the right one, that is, that when new commitments are undertaken their application may properly be limited to those ready to participate. Apart from the matter of equity or, in the customary GATT usage, "balance," the extent of progress on the non-tariff front will likely depend on the possibility of selective application. We assume, of course, that any new agreements on non-tariff measures would be open to any country prepared to accept their terms.

It is apparent that any serious forward movement on non-tariff measures will call for a stronger GATT. The not always crystal clear language of the General Agreement will need to be given greater exactitude, at least in interpretation. New provisions may have to be added. Most important, something more will have to be done toward enforcement, or toward effectively resolving disputes. We shall return to this subject in considering GATT reform.

VI. Export Controls and Scarce Supplies

Article 11 of the GATT bans quotas or other restrictions (aside from taxes) on exports as well as on imports.* It exempts from this stricture, however, "export prohibitions or restrictions temporarily applied to prevent critical shortages of foodstuffs or other products essential to the exporting contracting party." The exemption reflected postwar circumstances. Its authors did not anticipate the application of export limitations on anti-inflationary grounds, nor did they foresee politically motivated export controls. The question now is how to expand on Article 11 to deal with the widespread resort to restrictions on exports.

For the withholding of petroleum by the Arab producers and the earlier American restrictions on soybean exports are only the most publicized of the applications of this non-tariff obstacle to trade. At present, the United States has controls and the EC a virtual embargo on exports of scrap steel. Exports of cereals are embargoed or limited by a number of countries. As the American government lifts wage and price controls it asks for commitments from the exempted industries to limit their exports. There are many other examples.

It is necessary to distinguish between the different motivations for the application of export controls. One is straightforwardly political, as stated by the Arab nations in relating the volume of oil shipments to the Arab-Israel dispute. Another, of which oil may come to be representative, is a drive to raise prices by cartel action. A third, and currently the common one, is to try to transfer inflationary pressures to foreign customers by diverting intended export shipments back to the domestic market.

Political boycotts and cartel actions unquestionably present grave challenges to an inherently interdependent community. If normal economic life in large parts of the world can be held hostage to the arbitrary decisions of a few suppliers, then the outlook for a durable international order cannot be bright. At the same time, we have only a meager basis for judging the seriousness of this threat. For many primary goods, at any rate, cartels are likely to be difficult to organize

---

*Article 20 allows measures "essential to the acquisition or distribution of products in general or local short supply" provided they are applied equitably, but it seems clear from the record that this was intended to be applicable to special and transitional situations of the early postwar period and that Article 11 is the relevant one.

or to sustain. But the temptation to try to enforce high prices by restrictions on supply certainly will be present, and politically-grounded measures are always possible.

At least for oil, the prudent supposition must be that the consuming nations will have to live indefinitely with the hazard that their imports in the last analysis are vulnerable to the actions of the major producers. But the current phase, which developed out of circumstances of extraordinary political tension, does not give us the best grounds for judging the future. If the consumers can succeed in reducing wasteful uses of oil and can act together in any degree on increasing alternative energy sources, a more tolerable short-run balance will come into being. While this is going on, a careful assessment can be made of the ways in which the great trading nations can cope with future threats of supply interruptions.

A first and essential step, in any event, is to act to restore order among the industrial countries in respect of export control policy. If literally no rules apply as between the United States, the Community, and Japan, it would be odd to expect that other nations, GATT contracting parties or not, will be prepared to observe limits on their freedom of action. A minimum would be to further interpret Article 11 to require full advance consultation before export controls are applied and to write into it the principle that short supplies will be shared between exporters and their usual customers. It may be too much to suppose that the world is ready for mandatory sharing (for some foodstuffs and agricultural goods, however, stockpiling arrangements would serve to assure supplies), but an unambiguous advance consultation provision, if coupled with improved dispute resolution procedures in the GATT, would go a way toward bringing scarce supply restraints under multilateral control.

Whether or not such an example would be salutary with the non-industrial nations is not certain, but it could scarcely be unhelpful. Also, as will be noted in a subsequent section on trade with the developing countries, a fresh look at commodity agreements is in order. If such agreements could be negotiated, supply assurance provisions would normally be included.

VII.   SAFEGUARDS AGAINST
IMPORT DISRUPTION

For some time now, most especially but not only in the United States, discussions of trade policy have given much attention to finding a formula that would both enable countries to contain "disruptive" flows of imports and at the same time put limits on national freedom to raise and maintain protective barriers of an ostensibly emergency character. This interest in what have come to be called "safeguards" no doubt was heightened by Japan's extraordinary export surge in the late 1960's. More fundamental reasons may have been found in the growth of world trade in manufactures: an average annual rate of 13 percent, 1962-72, with exports of manufactures from developing to developed countries growing even more rapidly. Although no significant industries have anywhere been overwhelmed by import competition, adjustment problems of some severity have appeared from time to time. And the GATT safeguard provision, Article 19, has proved to be lacking, either as a satisfactory answer to genuine problems of short term adjustment or as a deterrent to the potential abuse of emergency import restrictions. There may well be substance, therefore, in the assertion that further liberalization of trade will depend on improving the international safeguard mechanism.

Article 19 sensibly allows import restricting measures in the event of actual or threatened "serious injury" to domestic producers, subject except in critical circumstances to a requirement of notification and consultation and in all cases to the rule of non-discrimination. It is of course not conceivable that any set of international commercial rules could be established without such an escape clause to deal with unforeseen situations. The difficulties with Article 19 have been not with the concept but with its application and even more its applicability.

In one part, the Article provides that exporting countries affected by emergency protective measures may withdraw trade concessions to balance the accounts, or alternatively, as the Article has been interpreted, that the restricting party may compensate for his action by offering concessions on other products. These can be powerful sanctions, but they can be difficult to enforce. If a number of exporting countries are involved, for example, suitable balancing concessions for each may be impossible to arrange. Or when import volumes are large, as was true for the American steel industry when it asked for protective action in the 1960's, claims to balancing actions may exceed anything that is feasible, or even desirable if the choice is to retaliate. The international arrangement on trade in cotton textiles, now extended to all textiles, was an early and major evasion of the GATT retaliation/compensation provision, and of its no discrimination rule as well. Disruption of textile markets, it was argued, was to be ascribed to low-wage countries, not to all exporters, and thus Article 19's MFN clause could not be applied, any more than, realistically, compensation in the amounts at issue could be paid.

The other side of the story is that once an Article 19 restriction has been imposed, the GATT has no clause requiring that the claim of injury periodically be reviewed, or that concessions be restored. If compensatory arrangements are made, the matter is settled. If not, under the Article all claims are considered waived after three months. And restrictions imposed outside Article 19's purview obviously are not likely to be submitted to GATT examination, once in force.

In spite of Article 19's shortcomings, however, it is not so simple to prescribe changes. Each country's right to emergency protection must be recognized, as in the present text. The principle of compensatory action, or retaliation, is also important, for the GATT is above all a charter based on the notion of reciprocity; indeed, with or without the authority of the General Agreement, the contracting parties will retain the ultimate possibility of reacting to other people's restrictions by compensatory measures.

We think, therefore, that the most promising approach is not through a revision of Article 19, which is surely impracticable anyway under the GATT voting rules, but through a protocol or interpretive note which could be subscribed to by all the contracting parties willing to give more detailed meaning to the existing Article. The 1972 proposal of an OECD high level group, under the chairmanship of Jean Rey, was along these lines. In effect, it would recommit the participants to a multilateral escape clause procedure. It would take as principles that emergency protection should be temporary under a preestablished time limit in each case, that new restrictive measures would allow for reasonable growth from the import level at the time of their application, and that the country using such measures would be expected to undertake domestic actions to help the adjustment of its affected industry. M. Rey and his colleagues would allow departures from MFN treatment in "exceptional" cases but only within the framework of multilateral procedures. Finally, they would establish a permanent panel of mediators in the GATT. Governments would bind themselves to turn to the mediators for advisory opinions on request of either another contracting party or the Director-General.

It seems to us that such an addition to the present Article 19 would provide both the flexibility that clearly must be available in emergency situations and a badly needed restatement of the common interest in protective measures taken by any trading nation. In particular, we believe that the proposed mediation body would be a most desirable extension of the GATT's institutional structure. We have noticed that the newly negotiated Arrangement Regarding International Trade in Textiles provides for the creation of a Textile Surveillance Body with powers of a mediatory nature. While the Arrangement sets up a highly special regime for the textile trade, the Surveillance Body holds promise of introducing into its operation a degree of multilateral judgment and control that has heretofore been lacking. It is not a prototype for a safeguards panel, but it does strongly suggest that the time has come for adding a mediation element to the GATT itself.

VIII.   GATT Reform

In earlier sections we have considered a number of issues which call into serious question the adequacy of the General Agreement as a charter of rules and obligations and as an institution for the international trading system as it is today. The General Agreement came into being in 1948 as a provisional treaty, embodying the bulk of the commercial policy provisions that had been drafted for the stillborn International Trade Organization. It is still provisional: its articles do not supersede national legislation that is inconsistent with obligations under the GATT. Its original twenty-three Contracting Parties have increased to more than eighty; with voting on a one country-one vote principle, the chief trading nations share in GATT decisions equally with all others, including a majority of members who do not or cannot apply GATT rules to their trade. Amendments require either a two-thirds or a unanimous vote. Effective procedures for the settlement of disputes are lacking and many issues consequently have been left unresolved for years. These and other weaknesses and shortcomings have not prevented the GATT from serving the international community honorably and well. But as the discussion thus far makes evident, the basic charter will have to be expanded upon if the GATT is adequately to serve present-day needs.

Thus an agricultural agreement along the lines we have suggested would call for the equivalent of a new GATT chapter and, undoubtedly, for a new consultative body as well. Action on the range of non-tariff measures, including export controls, would require detailed interpretations of the relative GATT articles and new provisions as well. A revamped safeguard provision could mean a protocol to Article 19 and, as we have seen, a permanent mediating body within the GATT.

It is possible to foresee a patchwork of new provisions, interpretations and clarifications of old provisions, and structural additions, amounting to a significant body of change in the General Agreement and its Geneva institution. On any assessment, only a fraction of the contracting parties would accept the additional obligations entailed by these changes. There would be added to the present text supplementary provisions or annexes, most of them limited in their terms to those willing to adhere to them. The adherents necessarily would include the major countries, for most new commitments or obligations of substance could win acceptance only if all of the principal trading nations (the Western European countries, the United States, Canada, Australia, and

Japan) acted together. It is most doubtful that the developing countries would be willing to assume these greater obligations.

Would it be desirable directly to combine the new commitments in a supplementary Code for the industrial members of GATT? We believe that it would. The voting and amending procedures of the General Agreement are formidable obstacles to membership-wide action, however much it may be needed. If the GATT is to be made a more responsive instrument in today's circumstances, changes will have to come through a different process, that is, through special arrangements mainly among the industrial countries. These could be codified under a separate charter in which voting power would correspond, at least more nearly, to the economic strength and responsibilities of the adherents. Suitable policy making bodies could be established, along with a special dispute resolution body (an Article 19 mediation panel could be given authority to mediate all trade disputes arising among the adherents to the Code). In the course of developing the Code, some inconsistent national laws would likely be overridden by new commitments, thereby modifying the provisional character of the GATT.

A code supplementing the GATT would need to be open to any nation ready to accept its commitments and obligations. Furthermore, Code members would continue to be bound by the general provisions of the GATT, including the most-favored-nation clause in Article 1. If the Code enabled the industrial countries to move more rapidly in reducing barriers to trade, the trading world as a whole would benefit. Nonetheless, the establishment of a separate charter, with its own institutional structure undoubtedly would arouse opposition among the large number of contracting parties not now prepared to participate. Whether this attitude could be dealt with should depend in largest part upon the extent to which the genuine trade interests of the developing countries are adequately taken into account by the industrial nations. We therefore consider this question next.

IX. TRADE NEGOTIATIONS AND THE DEVELOPING COUNTRIES

The Tokyo Declaration is replete with references to the special interests of the developing countries, whose spokesmen indeed comprised the overwhelming majority of the more than 100 nations represented. Taken all together, the Declaration gives negotiating priority to the products of the developing world, with concessions to be made by the industrial countries on a basis of less than reciprocity. The Generalized System of Preference is to be maintained and improved. And, "wherever appropriate," measures are to be taken to achieve stable, equitable, and remunerative prices for primary products, which is to be taken as a call for the negotiation of commodity agreements.

The emphasis of the Declaration is unexceptionable. Much of what it says is already contained in Part IV of the GATT, negotiated in 1965. If a new trade round is to be anything more than another expression of good intentions, the claims of the poor and poorest members of the community must be recognized in actions. There is, to be sure, a danger that the developing countries could make of the negotiations a grand debating session, as has been the standard pattern of the United Nations Conference on Trade and Development, rather than a conscientious and often tedious effort to find workable answers to hard questions. This risk avoided, however, the negotiating process should be able to give serious consideration to the preoccupations of the developing countries.

A special effort could be mounted to identify for tariff reductions — wherever possible to zero level — products of special interest to the developing countries. The General Preference schemes could be improved; assuming that the United States and Canada will be prepared to install their preferential arrangements, the negotiation could aim to expand the effective coverage of all the schemes. "Reverse" tariff preferences given to the Community by some developing countries may be an issue here, but all indications are that it is in process of disappearing anyway. Most important for the developing world as a whole, however, will be the depth and breadth of MFN reductions in tariffs and other relevant impediments to trade in manufactures generally. These will be concessions of a durable kind, which exporters and investors in the developing countries can rely upon to be maintained in most circumstances, for the industrial countries will usually have an equal interest in seeing to it that they are not withdrawn arbitrarily.

Reference to commodity agreements in the Tokyo Declaration raises immediately the question of their negotiability and their practicability. Experience with such arrangements — for example, in coffee, cocoa, sugar, tin, and wheat — shows that they are extremely difficult to negotiate, and difficult to operate as well. Any doctrinaire — pro or con — view of the present prospects ought, however, to be waived in favor of a reexamination of the commodity scene. As prices begin to fall from their peak levels, opportunities may present themselves for negotiations involving assurances of supply against assurances on floor prices. Petroleum of course could be the outstanding case in point. A time is likely to come within the next few years when oil producers and consumers alike will see benefits in an agreement that would offer stability to both sides. For this critical commodity at any rate, the virtues of potential stability of prices and supplies might well outweigh the disadvantages of additional governmental intervention in the world oil market.

Finally, there is the problem of food reserves for the third world. The Food and Agriculture Organization has done yeoman service in pointing out the tenuous food situation in many developing countries and in making the case for building or rebuilding food stocks against potential famine. It is only realistic, however, to recognize that if such stocks are to be created, the necessary financing for them will have to come in whole or part from the industrial countries; and that the negotiation may be most feasible within a negotiation on agricultural trade under the GATT. Specifically, if the United States, Canada, Australia, the Community, and Japan are going to consider a stockpiling system for the commercial trade in cereals and other products, the overlapping issue of famine stocks must be faced. It is a priority matter, and will have to be taken up in any case. But it probably can best be negotiated in a GATT context, where the whole range of agricultural trade questions can be examined in a search for practical answers.

ENERGY: THE IMPERATIVE FOR

A TRILATERAL APPROACH

John C. Campbell
*Senior
Research Fellow,
Council on
Foreign Relations*

Guy de Carmoy
*Professor,
European Institute
of Business
Administration,
Fontainebleau*

Shinichi Kondo
*Former
Ambassador
of Japan
to Canada*

99

Table of Contents

Energy: The Imperative for a Trilateral Approach

I. THE SCOPE OF THE PROBLEM

The energy crisis confronting the nations of Western Europe, North America and Japan is both specific and general, immediate and long-range. In its simplest and most urgent form it concerns the shortages of supply and the staggering increases in the price of oil with which each country has had to contend within the past year. More broadly, it has to do with shocks which these developments and our governments' attempts to cope with them may inflict on the world's monetary and trading system. And in the longer run the crisis poses fundamental questions about how our expanding industrial societies, which in the past quarter century have been fuelled increasingly by cheap and plentiful oil, will fare in the coming decade when oil supplies are neither cheap nor secure, and in the more distant future when they have virtually disappeared.

The war of October 1973 in the Middle East and its accompaniment of embargoes, cutbacks in oil production, and rises in price did not create the energy problem. These events speeded up trends already visible, gave them a sharp political twist, and revealed with merciless clarity the vulnerability of the industrial countries. It was evident that these countries could not go on indefinitely at the rate at which their consumption of energy had been expanding since 1950. Such further expansion would have to come mainly from imported oil, its availability uncertain and its price inordinately high.

The pervasive influence of the energy crisis on the entire fabric of national and international economic life will inevitably have political consequences and will require hard political decisions. Hence the importance, for the governments and peoples of the Trilateral countries, of seeing the magnitude and scope of the problem. When they see it, we believe they will find no viable alternative to a common approach.

This report first examines the economics of the future energy picture, then the politics of it, and finally makes some proposals. These proposals are not a panoply of detailed policy recommendations. We considered it more important at this stage to establish common purposes and set the general directions for policy.

A. ECONOMICS

It is useful to distinguish two time perspectives, one for the next ten years or so, and the other running to the end of this century and into the next.

In the first period the economy of the industrialized Trilateral region as a whole will continue to be dependent on oil imports from OPEC (Organization of Petroleum Exporting Countries) sources. Our societies are based on high energy consumption. They cannot suffer a drastic drop in available supply or stagnation in the rate of energy growth without serious economic and social consequences. Against this structural demand there is an insufficiency of reliable supply, since a critical part of our current supply is subject to decisions on access and on price which are out of our control and can be arbitrarily made. Because substitute sources of supply will take years to develop, the period of continued dependence will last into the 1980's for virtually all the Trilateral countries and beyond 1985 for most of them.

The world's supply of oil is sufficient to meet all import requirements over the next ten years. There could even be a surplus, provided the OPEC countries continue to export and the consuming countries take effective measures of conservation and successfully pursue the development of oil in non-OPEC countries as well as of other sources of energy. Whether imports are adequate will largely depend on the policies of OPEC countries, which will be determined by such factors as need for revenue, the price trend, investment opportunities and political motivation.

Also crucial in gauging possible shortfalls of supply is estimated growth in requirements for imported oil. Projections made in the early 1970's, based on what had been normal rates of growth in energy consumption during the two previous decades, set U.S. import requirements in 1985 in the vicinity of 13 million barrels per day, Western Europe's at about 23 million, and Japan's at about 11 million. All three regions, in those circumstances, would be increasingly and critically dependent on imports, which would have to come mainly from the Middle East. As a result of experience and further study since the autumn of 1973, such projections can be revised to take account of anticipated conservation, greater efficiency in energy use, increased domestic production of oil, gas, and coal, and higher prices. Much more can be accomplished by such measures in the United States, however, than in Europe or Japan. U.S. import requirements might be reduced to less than 5 million b/d, perhaps as little as 3 million, by 1985 or even by 1980. Western Europe's imports would still be between 15 and 20 million b/d, Japan's between 9 and 10 million.

The question of price may be even more difficult, for the drastic rise in prices determined by OPEC at the end of 1973 inevitably upset the economic equilibrium of the consuming countries and foreordained a massive transfer of financial assets, and thus of economic power, from them to the oil-producing countries. The anticipated additional oil bill, for 1974 alone, will be about $40 to $50 billion for the industrial countries and $10 billion for the developing countries unfortunate enough not to be exporters of oil. The effects on the international monetary system, on currency values, on rates of inflation, on food and fertilizer production, and on living standards are impossible to calculate but bound to impose strains of an unprecedented character.

Looking well beyond the immediate problems and those of the next decade, we can see the end of the hydrocarbon age. The date cannot be fixed because the size of new discoveries of oil and gas cannot be predicted, but with consumption outrunning additions to proved reserves the handwriting is on the wall. The world must be prepared, accordingly, to make the transition 40 or 50 years hence to an economy based primarily on coal (and its derivatives) and on nuclear power. The goal will be to reach, without a disastrous gap, the age when abundant renewable energy is available for the world's use through new methods such as breeder reactors, controlled nuclear fusion, or harnessing the power of the sun. The conditioning factors for supply of energy over the long term are investment, technology, and ecology, and the initial decisions have to be made now.

The economic problems may seem simple — how to restrain demand and maximize supply at tolerable cost and where to put investment in alternatives to oil — but in fact are complex because they combine short, medium, and long-term considerations and at the same time involve a balancing of financial, technological and other factors. They will require on the part of our governments considered and far-reaching decisions, which should serve to promote international interests rather than merely to satisfy short-term national interests.

B. POLITICS

In bringing the world through the next decade and the transition to new forms of energy without major upheavals, the advanced industrial societies of North America, Europe and Japan have a deep involvement and special responsibilities. With economies which are interdependent and political interests which in the past have been compatible and mutually supporting, they have an overriding concern with the good health of relations among themselves and with the preservation of a workable trading system and an effective international monetary structure, both of which are already under stress.

It seems clear that international economic relations, with a strong assist from the energy crisis, will take on an increasingly political character. This is already apparent in the relations between oil-consuming and oil-producing states. The private oil companies, where they have not already been taken over, can no longer make decisions to the extent heretofore on such matters as how much they will produce in producing states or at what price. The governments of consuming countries do not have much to say about those matters either, but they know now that getting oil is their problem and that they have to deal with it both in discussions with each other and in negotiations with producing states.

How are the OPEC members, mainly the big Persian Gulf producers, to be persuaded to keep up the supplies of oil? All of them know that their oil reserves are finite. They will decide for themselves on the rate at which their reserves will be used. Some, with major economic development programs, may prefer a high level of oil exports in order to maintain a high level of income. Others, with smaller populations and less ambitious programs, may be reluctant to push production beyond the point which meets their own needs for money income. Some may restrict production in order to prolong the life of their reserves. All will wish to keep prices well above the pre-1973 levels. And some may wish at one time or another to determine policy on production and export of oil on essentially political grounds. The partial relaxation of Arab embargoes and production cutbacks early in 1974 was tactical rather than strategic; the Arab oil-producing states have said that they will use the "oil weapon" again if they find it necessary.

Similarly in the case of relations with the less developed countries which are not oil-producers, the effects of the energy crisis will bring governments of the Trilateral countries, by choice or by circumstance, into increasing involvement in international economic relations. The rise in oil prices threatens the world's poorer countries with economic ruin, and resultant social and political upheaval. They will seek to avert such a disaster by mobilizing political pressure on the rest of the world for massive concessional aid and by trying to apply the OPEC method to any valued raw materials they themselves may have. The developed countries and the newly rich oil-producers will have to make basic political decisions on how to meet this situation.

The end of the era of cheap and plentiful energy is most striking, perhaps, in its impact within our own countries. One cannot predict how far-reaching the economic and social effects will be. Inflation, industrial slowdown and unemployment may bring social unrest, further loss of confidence in governments, and political disorder. What is more easily predictable is that under these multifarious dislocations and pressures the lines between private decision and public control, between the freedom of individuals to live their own lives and the social requirement for rationality and equity in the use of scarce resources, will come under strain. These are practical rather than philosophical questions. They will challenge the ability of our societies to maintain democratic institutions and the essentials of free enterprise necessary to an efficient economy.

Over the long run, the energy problem poses fundamental questions about rates of growth, conservation of resources, the balance between economic and environmental values, and the creation or refashioning of institutional structures adequate to the challenge of new demands. Within national economies, under pressure of high-cost energy, governments and peoples will have to take decisions on allocation of resources, on priorities among different forms of production and subsidies to investment, on revamping of transportation systems, and on patterns of location for industry, public services, and housing.

These are, in the common view, problems of domestic policy, and we do not pretend to judge how each country should proceed in dealing with them. But the line between domestic and foreign policy is unclear, and the inclination is always present to have the cost paid by someone else. At such a time it will require extraordinary leadership on the part of governments, as well as extraordinary public understanding and discipline, to avoid seemingly simple solutions which promise, in the short run, more imported oil or higher exports or a cheaper currency. For such a course will lead only to destructive competition in scrambling for oil, pushing exports and shutting off imports, and devaluing currencies.

It is hard to avoid the conclusion that the greatest challenge of the energy crisis lies in the relations among the developed nations of the Trilateral region. Thus far it has done more to disrupt the European Community than to pull it together. Restrictive measures taken by Italy under severe economic pressure may be followed by similar moves by other states, setting in motion a serious disintegrating trend in the E.E.C. Energy questions have also strained Europe's and Japan's relations with the United States. Unless these nations can establish the necessary cooperation with each other, they can hardly be effective in dealing with the rest of the world, the oil-producing countries especially. In order to have a realistic basis for such collaboration, it is necessary to see what the respective positions of the different Trilateral countries are and what are the factors of competition and of common interest to be taken into account.

C. RELATIVE POSITIONS OF THE THREE REGIONS

The balance among the three regions should be conceived first of all in terms of energy resources, but also in terms of political and military influence, economic and monetary strength, and technological capabilities.

The position of North America is relatively strong. The United States and Canada have very large potential resources (oil, natural gas, coal, oil shale, tar sands) which if developed could produce energy well beyond their own needs. The United States will not be critically dependent on Middle East oil, which made up only 6 percent of primary energy consumption in 1973, unless it allows the whole of its increment in energy growth to come from that source. It has the natural resources, the financial means, the technological capacity and presumably the political will to become virtually self-sufficient in energy by 1985 and to remain so. The net supplementary cost of oil imports may amount to $10 billion in 1974, but the balance on current account with the oil-producing countries may improve considerably within the next few years because of their desire for American goods. Moreover, the attractiveness of the American market for long-term investments should increase capital inflows. The dollar is emerging from the energy crisis stronger than before.

Canada is roughly self-sufficient in energy now (imports of oil to eastern Canada in the past were generally matched by exports from western Canada) and may remain so. Although Alberta's conventional oil sources will taper off, they may eventually be more than replaced by oil and gas from the Arctic and oil from the Athabasca tar sands. Canadian governments of whatever political stripe are likely to be developing a national energy policy carefully attuned to Canada's needs, and to be chary of any rapid exploitation of its resources by foreign capital largely for foreign markets.

The United States is the strong partner in the Atlantic alliance and in its security arrangements with Japan. Its naval power in the Mediterranean and the Indian Ocean is the only military counterweight to Soviet power in those areas. It is the main supplier of arms to Israel, Jordan, Iran, and other Middle East countries and is regarded by a number of those states as a mainstay of their security. The United States also has considerable political and diplomatic leverage in the Arab-Israeli conflict through its influence with both sides. Although its policies of support for Israel have tended in the past to undermine its relations with the Arab states, including the oil-producers, its success in arranging interim settlements between that country and Egypt and Syria has strengthened its position in the area as a whole.

Western Europe is in a much weaker position, both politically and in respect of energy. Although the E.E.C. functions as a common trading unit, it lacks strong political institutions. Neither the Community nor its member states have significant military influence in the Middle East. They have an interest in a peaceful settlement of the Arab-Israeli conflict but have not been able to play an effective part in bringing it about through negotiation.

The dominant fact of Western Europe's energy situation is its dependence on Middle East oil (60 percent of O.E.C.D. Europe's primary energy consumption in 1973). This proportion may be somewhat reduced in the next decade through the development of North Sea oil and gas and the pursuit of strict and consistent policies on the use of energy, but it is doubtful that dependence on external supplies will be brought below 45 percent by 1985. This relatively weak position is accentuated by the absence of a common energy policy in the E.E.C. and by the tendency of individual governments to act on their own in matters crucial to each other's welfare. One has therefore to consider separately the positions and policies of individual European countries.

Great Britain and the Federal Republic of Germany are about 50 percent self-sufficient in primary energy consumption, while France and Italy are about 80 percent dependent. Britain will have difficulty in the next few years in meeting its oil import bill at a time of serious balance-of-payments difficulties and uncertainty over continued membership in the E.E.C., but its longer-term prospects are favorable because of North Sea oil and gas. Germany, at least in the short term, can balance its trade in spite of the high cost of oil thanks to its formidable export potential and large monetary reserves; but Germany may lose export markets as other countries take defensive measures to protect their own industries and pay for imported oil.

France is faced with large trade deficits, is investing heavily in nuclear plants, and has resorted to substantial external borrowing. Its position is essentially weak despite some positive elements such as comparatively large gold reserves (which will jump in value if there is a revaluation at or around the market price), heavy sales of arms to oil-producing countries, and a pro-Arab foreign policy that might win special favors. The plight of Italy is the most serious. Unable to stop the drain on its balance of payments despite heavy borrowing, it has introduced import restrictions to the detriment of its partners in the E.E.C. as a short-term palliative measure. Italy's fundamental problems remain unsolved, and its situation is likely to get worse.

Europe thus faces a bleak prospect. The increase in its oil import bill for 1974 is estimated at $22 billion. With the exception of Germany and perhaps the Netherlands, the E.E.C. countries face the alternatives of (a) accepting a marked depreciation of their currencies, (b) resorting to external borrowing at unprecedented levels, or (c) reducing drastically their imports of energy and of non-essentials. They will probably combine all three, and the end result could be a monetary collapse.

Japan is more dependent than Western Europe as a whole on external supplies of energy — about 86 percent of domestic consumption. All of its petroleum is imported, over 80 percent of it from the Middle East. Thus Japan is the most vulnerable of all the industrial nations and does not expect the major international oil companies to be able to guarantee the needed volume of supplies. High prices for oil (the import bill is likely to increase by $8-10 billion in 1974) have already led to a weakening of its previously strong trading position, depreciation of the currency, and a further rise in inflation. Its ability to continue meeting its oil bill will depend on its long-range export possibilities and on the survival of the world free trading system. Japan will try to develop its domestic energy resources, principally nuclear energy, as well as to diversify its external sources of supply, but it cannot escape from its position of dependence on and vulnerability to overseas supply. Therefore, it is vitally important for Japan to maintain and develop cooperative relations with oil-producing countries. However, Japan has not held such political and military leverage in the Middle East as have the

United States and, in lesser degree, some of the Western European countries.

For any and all of the oil-consuming countries, the prospect of massive exports to producing countries is very attractive, as is the idea of getting back as investment the funds they pay out for oil. They are, however, in competition with each other in exports and in attracting investments, and those in the stronger positions are likely to have the advantage. Thus the United States has an edge in the selling of arms, for reasons of technology and political influence. Germany and Japan have the best possibilities for selling equipment. And investments of oil money from the Middle East are more likely to flow to America or Germany than to countries with weaker currencies and dimmer prospects. The absence of strong European institutions, mainly an economic and monetary union, works against the recycling of funds to Europe.

This factual picture of differing economic and financial positions of the countries and regions of the Trilateral area must be understood both for its political reality and for its disturbing implications. For some years ahead the United States, Canada, and later Great Britain will feel a certain confidence in the possession of energy resources which the others will not have. Germany and Japan may have compensating advantages in the competitive strength of their economies. Intensive competition, if it is uncontrolled, can turn out very badly for those in a weaker position. Competition should therefore be matched by cooperation.

Cooperation, of course, has its limits; for example, it cannot determine where Arab investors will put their money or to whom private bankers will make loans. The stronger countries will not be inclined to engage in an unending series of operations to rescue the weaker. Yet all have a stake in the survival of all, and in the survival of a viable economic order in the world. The United States could not be indifferent to a monetary collapse in Europe. In the framework of a long-term approach which makes sense for all, which offers a constructive alternative to the uncertainty and vulnerability of the period immediately ahead, it becomes politically possible and indeed necessary for the stronger economies to aid the weaker, provided the latter, through conservation of energy and in other ways, are pulling their weight and not merely getting a free ride.

II. THE NEED FOR COOPERATION

The Trilateral countries should go forward together in a joint commitment to develop energy and to meet its high cost, with a plan covering the next 20 years or so. They will not succeed if they have conflicting strategies.

The energy problem requires not only a series of defensive measures against shortage, dislocation, inflation, and the excesses of economic nationalism, but also a positive strategy which sets priorities and assures the rational, long-term development of energy resources in ways compatible with democratic freedoms. Market forces will provide much of the motive power, but it is necessary to set the context within which private decisions on investment, for example, can be made and market forces can operate to the best advantage. The overall strategy must take the form of public policy based on the conscious choice and dedicated effort of governments and peoples, first of all among the advanced industrial nations but with full consideration for the interests of other nations and an open invitation for their cooperation.

At the Washington conference of February 1974 the countries of the three regions (except France) agreed on the need for "a comprehensive action program to deal with all facets of the world energy situation by cooperative measures." Based on that agreement a coordinating group was established, and work goes forward in the O.E.C.D. and in ad hoc working groups. It is not our purpose here to review or to judge this work· in its present early stages. This report will concentrate on the overall approach to the problem, the need to establish long-term goals, and the specific fields in which early and effective action is essential.

A. CONSERVATION AND EFFICIENT USE OF ENERGY

The consuming countries should intensify and coordinate their efforts for the more efficient use of energy, setting specific targets and working out plans for investment, technology and public policy to achieve them.

We stress this subject both for its promise of actual results and for its important psychological effects. Avoidance of waste and increasing efficiency in the use of energy are mandatory in an age of scarcity and high cost, when many systems and methods unattractive at earlier prices become feasible and desirable. Much can be done without changing lifestyles, and more can be done with some changes. Extravagance in personal consumption is no essential attribute of a free society; indeed, to trim unnecessary fat may have social as well as economic benefits. Economic incentive will provide the main motivation, but governments will have to set priorities for the use of energy, limit the consumption of certain goods, engage in planning, pass legislation, and vote funds in such fields as mass transit.

We should recognize that the consumption of energy cannot be expected or permitted to grow exponentially, as it has in the past, at a rate which would project a doubling of U.S. demand between 1970 and 1985, and a doubling again by 2000, and even higher rates of growth for Europe and Japan. Holding down demand for energy is one of the surest ways, within its limits, of coping with the problem of supply. Some measures can be taken at once, without heavy investment. In other cases, investment in efficiency of use will be much less than the investment in a corresponding increase in supply, and the return will often be more rapid. Conservation is also a method which gives rise to a minimum of international controversy and can induce habits of cooperation. Improvements in energy efficiency should be widely applicable in industry, transportation, housing, and electric power production, with much of the cooperation carried out by private firms and research organizations. Joint research should go forward with both public and private support.

Obviously, demand cannot be cut in the same precise proportions in each country. Geographic, economic and social factors differ. Japan is under greater pressure to save energy than the United States or Canada, but has less margin for doing so. Ten percent saving from past levels of consumption is within reach of all. Although formal international agreement on fixed standards of conservation would be hard to attain and probably not necessary, governments should nevertheless set generally agreed targets, which would not necessarily be the same for each country. Without roughly comparable levels of effort it will be difficult to have an effective sharing of supplies in an emergency.

B. ASSURING SAFE AND ADEQUATE SUPPLIES

To assure adequate supplies, our nations will have to find the most effective combination of bargaining power and mutual interest to encourage the continued availability of OPEC oil over the next decade, and will have to take as soon as possible the initial decisions on development

*of alternative sources of energy elsewhere, especially in
the Trilateral countries themselves.*

Here there is a double set of problems. The first involves measures
to develop supplies within the Trilateral area itself and in areas deemed
relatively safe from interruption. The second involves doing what is
possible to assure the continued flow of oil from the principal exporting countries now members of OPEC. The two problems are related
in that progress toward self-sufficiency and in broadening the base of
supplies narrows the market for OPEC oil and may increase the incentives for continuing to supply it. Yet economic bargaining power on
the consumer side will still be limited owing to the quasi-monopoly
position of the producers. The consuming countries should offer all the
incentives they reasonably can, such as the sale of capital equipment
and technical skills for development programs, or investment in projects
outside national borders for those like Saudi Arabia with income-earn-
ing capacity surplus to their own needs for development.

Such arrangements cannot guarantee the continued flow of oil
imports, especially if political developments in the Middle East bring
Arab states once more to the use of the "oil weapon." The consumers
will have the best chance of coping with all contingencies if they maintain solidarity among themselves both to set the framework of cooperation with the producing states and to face cutbacks and embargoes if
and when they are imposed. The producing states should know that to
cause economic breakdown in the industrial countries by withholding
supplies or by sky-high prices cannot be in their own interest, and that
economic relations must be seen in the context of overall political and
security interests on both sides.

In the interest of larger and more diverse supplies, the consuming
countries, and in particular their oil companies, should look to the
possibilities of exploration and development of oil and gas in such areas
as offshore Asia, Africa, and South America, where the political hazards
may be lower than in the Middle East. Joint projects involving a number of governments and companies, working with the sovereign local
governments, might be the most promising approach. With Venezuela's
consent, a major endeavor of this kind to develop oil from the Orinoco
tar belt could be a boon to the world oil supply of the future.

Within the Trilateral area those countries with significant energy
resources should develop them. There will be a common interest in
having the United States move ahead with coal (including coal gasifi-

cation and liquefaction), oil shale, and additional oil and gas; Canada with Arctic gas and Athabasca tar sands; Britain and Norway with North Sea oil and gas; and all with nuclear energy. Whatever increases the total supply should benefit the entire community. There may be a common interest also in pursuing some of these endeavors in joint projects involving, for example, European and Japanese participation in development of coal resources in the United States, Canada and Australia, or U.S., European, and Japanese participation in the development of Canada's tar sands. The United States, Canada, Norway and Great Britain, primarily concerned with use of their resources in the light of their own long-term needs, may be reluctant to include others or to make commitments regarding future export of their resources. We believe, however, that they should allow outside participation in the development of resources and the freest possible marketing of energy products, taking due account of their own long-term requirements, especially since the resentments fed by unilateralism and dog-in-the-manger policies would adversely affect the spirit and practice of cooperation among the consumer countries.

The need for investment in all kinds of energy over periods up to 20 years is such that cooperation for reducing costs is essential, and joint planning is required to assure coordination of long-range policies. One cardinal point in respect of supply is that the industrial countries, having made the decision to develop high-cost energy as the alternative to and eventual replacement for imported oil, have to stick with their decision. They cannot relax, without heed for the morrow, at times when the oil is flowing in. Those who undertake the investments must have assurance that the projects will go on and the products will be marketed, even if the oil-producing states should drop their price below the level at which these products are to be sold.

C. SHARING IN AN EMERGENCY

Our governments should be prepared for a situation of enforced scarcity, and therefore should agree on (a) the conditions which will constitute an emergency; (b) a stockpiling program; (c) emergency production plans; (d) special conservation measures and (e) a plan for the allocation of supplies.

The experience in 1973-1974 showed that when an emergency occurs it is too late to establish an effective sharing plan. The private companies did well in the distribution of available supplies, but they did not seek that authority and do not want it in the future. To make a plan for the next such shortage is a concrete, feasible and necessary task which governments can perform now.

The sharing plan should be based on need, taking into account both consumption and import patterns. If the emergency is marked by embargoes or other discrimination on the part of producing countries in supplying oil, the sharing plan should have the effect of spreading on an agreed basis the consequences of such unequal treatment, even at the risk of further measures limiting the total supply. That idea may be difficult to apply in practice, but it should be accepted as a guiding principle. If the opposite concept of go-it-alone prevails in this field of energy policy, it will surely prevail in others as well.

D. THE FINANCIAL IMPACT

Action by governments and by international financial institutions will be needed to supplement the banking system in meeting the impact of increased oil prices on the economies of consuming countries and on the international monetary and trade structure.

Meeting the higher cost of imported oil is both an immediate and a long-term problem. It has no easily discernible solution. Short-term borrowing may get some importing countries through their immediate financial crises but merely puts off the day of reckoning. Industrial societies cannot cut oil imports drastically to fit their pocketbooks because the shock to their economies would reduce still further their ability to pay. They will do what they can do to increase exports to producing countries, but even the most rapid increases of imports by OPEC countries must lag far behind the explosive growth of their export earnings. In trade, as in the "recycling" of surplus funds through their investment in consuming countries, the money is not likely to flow through the banking system back to the countries which need it most. (This question is taken up in the special report of Richard N. Cooper, North American rapporteur of the Trilateral Monetary Task Force.)

The unavoidable result of the present high price for imported oil is that some countries of the Trilateral region will find great difficulty in paying for oil and their other needed imports over any extended period and may exhaust their credit. In the absence of cooperative efforts to ease their burden, there is a danger that they will be forced into nationalistic measures of import limitation, dumping, and currency devaluation, provoking retaliatory and competitive moves by other

114

countries. This is a situation of urgency requiring common approaches within the European Community and between the Community, the United States and Japan. They are already working out in the O.E.C.D. a code of good conduct. On the financial side, the nations which are financially stronger will have to help, by government guarantees of bank loans or in more direct ways, those threatened with crisis, or all will in time be in crisis.

Individually and in concert, the Trilateral countries must do what they can to combat the effects of high oil prices by all possible measures of conservation and import substitution. Yet as long as the dependence on imports for a vital portion of energy requirements exists, the producing countries can more or less set the price they want. Wishing their oil reserves to last, they will have a continuing interest in getting more money for less oil.

The possibilities of reduction in oil prices lie in (a) competition among producing states anxious to maximize income but unable to agree through OPEC on manipulating exports and prices to that end, or (b) recognition by the producers of the global consequences of depression and possible economic breakdown in the industrial countries. In such circumstances one or more of the major producers might agree to lower the price of oil or to accept a scheme for deferral of a portion of the payments. But the only sure way to be relieved of paying tribute to the producers is to proceed seriously with development of alternative sources of energy. This will be high-cost energy, of course, but probably not far from today's prices for OPEC oil, and in time it should establish a ceiling above which oil imports would not go. The demonstration of serious intent could have an effect on prices before the new sources were actually producing in quantity.

The effects of vast surplus OPEC funds on the world's money markets and on the international monetary system are potentially disruptive and complicate the task of reforming that system now in progress. These questions are beyond the scope of this report. We note them in order to emphasize the difficulty of getting an agreement on monetary policy unless there is also cooperation on energy policy.

E. TECHNOLOGY AND RESEARCH

The need for rapid progress in efficient use of energy, protection of the environment, and development of new resources will require a more extensive sharing of technology and more joint research.

If there is solidarity in the distribution of scarcity, there should be solidarity in the distribution of new technology to overcome scarcity. It is comparable to a wartime situation in which allied governments, in developing new weapons and in mobilizing their economies, put science and technology to work where there are the best chances for achieving results.

Priorities have to be established on the main lines of research and development in new forms of energy and the division of labor for pursuing them. Past experience highlights the difficulties of predicting the rate of the development of nuclear power, but by 1985 it could be producing at least 15 percent of total energy consumption in the O.E.C.D. countries. Thereafter, the world will count on the increasing use of nuclear power, but on many aspects — providing adequate fuel for nuclear plants, preventing diversion of fissionable materials, ensuring safety — technology must be developed further and political-economic decisions have to be made. These matters cannot be adequately dealt with on the national level alone.

Looking further ahead to forms of energy to which scientific discovery has not yet brought us (nuclear fusion, solar energy for electricity, hydrogen, and others), governments and research institutions will have to set priorities for the use of their talents and resources in accordance with a general plan, and to review and change those priorities as the march of science and technology goes forward.

Taking account of all these requirements, the United States, Canada, the E.E.C. and Japan should work out an agreement on cooperation in the field of energy research and development.

III. RELATIONS WITH OTHER COUNTRIES

A. OIL-PRODUCING COUNTRIES

The consuming countries must try, as indicated under the above recommendations on supply and on price, to build a continuing relationship with the oil-producing countries in which both sides have a stake and which they will not wish to disrupt.

It is not easy to create that relationship, given the atmosphere of the past year. The credibility gap is wide, but obviously the dialogue has to begin. Many of the producing countries' arguments are well taken and deserve a respectful hearing in the search for an accommodation of interests.

The new relationship, in any case, must take account of the legitimate desire of the producing nations to own and control their resources, to build industries to process those resources, to move rapidly ahead on the path of general development, and to make sound investments. It should accord to them a place in international economic councils commensurate with their increased economic status.

The industrial states should be prepared to furnish technology and management skills to help them diversify their economies, improve their agriculture, and prepare for the time when their oil resources will decline, for example, by joint research in the field of solar energy. Building refineries and petrochemical industries in the oil-producing countries will tend to increase dependence and to increase the cost of petroleum products for the consumers, but these industries are going to be built one way or another and the wise course is to help.

Solidarity of the consuming countries remains essential, as the alternative to a ruinous scramble for competitive advantage. This does not mean a confrontation of two monolithic blocs or a huge conference of consumers versus producers, but neither does it mean that the former should not use what bargaining power they possess, which in the overall picture of markets, trade, technology and investment is considerable. They should be in a position to use it flexibly, encouraging moderate policies on the part of producers.

Bilateral contacts or approaches to producing countries on a regional basis should not be ruled out as long as they do not have the effect of tying up supplies, bidding up prices to the detriment of others, or reducing the potential bargaining power of all consumers. If the E.E.C. is maintained as a customs union, of which a common energy policy is a necessary complement — and this is assumed to be in the general Trilateral interest — it must be expected to negotiate with the oil-producing countries on trade and investment, though not on prices. Such a regional approach may be beneficial and is clearly preferable to bilateralism on a national basis. Whether the producing states would engage in negotiations with the E.E.C. singly or as a group would be for them to decide; the former method seems more likely.

American, European and Japanese firms will be competing in exports to the oil-producing countries, but here again the general interests of the Trilateral countries as a whole should set the framework. The more bilateral deals are expanded, the more those who make them are subject to political pressure. Unrestricted and uncoordinated bilateral projects also tend to work in the direction of wild and uneconomic investment in the oil-producing region as a whole, which is in no party's interest. International consortia may be useful for many development projects, especially for large and politically conspicuous ones. At the least, there should be an accepted practice of exchanging information and consulting in the O.E.C.D.

Similarly on political matters, a generally agreed overall approach to such questions as settlement of the Arab-Israeli conflict or arms sales to Middle East states would increase the chances of harmonizing oil policy with political and security objectives. Our several governments would, of course, maintain their own respective interests and differing degrees of intimacy with the various Middle East states, but they must avoid the acrimony and cross purposes which characterized their mutual relations in the autumn of 1973. North America, Western Europe and Japan have common interests in the availability of Arab oil, in the survival of Israel, in Arab-Israeli peace settlements, and in a stable balance and the avoidance of great-power conflict in the region. All have a political-economic role to play in that area in the years ahead.

Although the United States as a superpower sees these problems with a broad strategic view, and Europe and Japan see them primarily from the standpoint of their vital interest in oil, harmony on broad policy is necessary not only in light of their own mutual relations, but also in bringing the Middle East states as well to see their policies on oil in the broader context of international security and cooperation. Therefore, there should be close and frequent consultation among the Trilateral countries on their broad policies in the Middle East.

B. THE SOVIET UNION AND CHINA

It is logical to explore possibilities of obtaining increased supplies of energy from the U.S.S.R. or China, but these possibilities do not offer the prospect of meeting any substantial part of the problem.

Proposals presently under discussion by U.S. and Japanese companies with the Soviet Government seem to involve high costs and high risks, and should be weighed against comparable investments elsewhere. Vast Soviet reserves of energy, particularly of natural gas, may indeed prove to be a much needed source in the 1980's for the U.S.S.R. itself and for many other countries as well. Increasing the supplies of Soviet gas to Europe appears to make more sense than costly and complex arrangements for shipment of liquefied natural gas to the United States. It is natural for Japan to diversify its sources of energy by looking both to the U.S.S.R. and to China (which is potentially a considerable oil exporter).

As for the general political aspects, Japan or European countries may be wise not to go into large-scale energy projects in the U.S.S.R. except in association with each other or with the United States. Cooperation in energy development with the Soviet Union or China could help to strengthen the trends drawing those countries more into the world economy, but none of the Trilateral countries should take the political risk of a substantial degree of energy dependence on the Soviet Union or China.

C. DEVELOPING COUNTRIES

Because the rise in oil prices, together with increased prices for other essential products, threatens a number of the developing countries with disaster, they should be afforded help both immediately and in the longer term.

Emergency aid must be furnished in the form of grants or soft loans, for there is little prospect that it can be repaid. The stronger industrial countries, especially those which have gained by the high prices of food, fertilizers and other goods needed by the developing countries, should maintain or increase current levels of aid despite their own troubles with oil payments, and the oil-producing countries should also contribute through existing international financial institutions or new arrangements such as have been proposed by Iran. It should be clear that this is not just the "north-south problem" in more acute form, for the oil-producing states have both a heavy responsibility for the plight of the others and ample means to ease it.

In the longer run, the continuance of high-cost energy for all will create for many developing countries a situation of permanent inability to meet their fuel bills. As the developed countries increase their own production of energy, there should be more Middle East oil available on the world market, perhaps at a lower price. One way or another, the prices the poorer developing countries pay for oil and for food will have to come down, or arrangements for concessional aid on a more or less permanent basis will have to be established. Because this is a common obligation of the industrial and the oil-producing countries, it provides another facet of the cooperation which their own reciprocal interests in oil, trade and development will require them to build. And the urgent human considerations for doing so should be beyond dispute.

IV. INSTITUTIONS

The Trilateral countries need adequate institutional arrangements to coordinate the many aspects of their joint and several approaches to the energy problem. There will have to be continuing consultation among governments, but regular diplomatic channels will not be adequate. If there is need for a general master plan or strategy setting the broad lines of policy, there is need for an organization where its adaptation to changing conditions and its translation into practice can be worked out.

The O.E.C.D., because of the character of its membership and its general function of setting and overseeing the rules of the game, provides the natural framework. An energy agency associated with the O.E.C.D., primarily a consulting body but with some delegated authority, would be a logical central institution for coordinating the tasks which have to be done, everything from current stockpiling to long-range plans for research. The important thing is not the label or the established procedures but the ability to get the job done. If the O.E.C.D. should be too cumbersome or prove inadequate as an action-oriented body, the possibility of a new energy agency representing Canada, the United States, the E.E.C., and Japan should be studied.

120

V. CONCLUSION

The energy crisis has propelled the industrial nations into a situation to which other factors were also bringing them though more slowly: a situation in which they have to set the lines of basic policy together or succumb to chaotic national competition and a destruction of the fundaments of a rational world order. The real challenge of the energy problem is not a struggle with outside adversaries, as in most great crises of the past, but within and among our respective societies. Our governments must provide bold and farsighted leadership in their domestic and foreign policies to face the challenge. Our peoples need a wartime psychology to fight this war against ourselves. They should be prepared to tighten their belts and to share sacrifices among themselves — because it will be a long, uphill struggle.

ENERGY: A STRATEGY FOR

INTERNATIONAL ACTION

John C. Campbell
*Senior
Research Fellow,
Council on
Foreign Relations*

Guy de Carmoy
*Professor,
European Institute
of Business
Administration,
Fontainebleau*

Shinichi Kondo
*Former
Ambassador
of Japan
to Canada*

Table of Contents

ENERGY: A STRATEGY
FOR INTERNATIONAL ACTION

Energy is the economic lifeblood of the industrialized nations. In the next decade, with the supply of energy uncertain and its cost high, they will face new and critical challenges dangerous to their economic and social stability and to their political institutions.

It is not a matter of energy economics alone, or of political decisions by individual governments on how to cope with shortage. Energy is central to the whole complex of international economic relations involving the supply and movement of raw materials, the rules and practices of world trade, the maintenance of an international monetary system, and the control of inflation. On the political side, the problems of supply and price have compelled the energy-consuming countries to find new kinds of relationships with the principal oil-exporting countries. Above all, and most important for our purposes here, the crisis brings inevitable stress within each consuming country and in their relations with each other. It has already weakened the fabric of the European Community and added strains to the ties between Europe, the United States, and Japan.*

In our previous report, *Energy: The Imperative for a Trilateral Approach,* we pointed out that our countries face a situation not unlike those of wartime, requiring a comparable degree of effort, cooperation, and willingness to share sacrifices among allies. Thus far, however, the best comparison is to the conduct of the Western democracies in the period of the "phony war" of 1939-40. The response of governments and peoples has been weak and inadequate. They have not shown that they have grasped the magnitude of the problem, much less defined with

---

*This report concentrates primarily on non-monetary aspects of the international implications of the energy crisis. A special memorandum on monetary aspects was presented to the Executive Committee meeting in June 1974 and additional materials were considered at the December 1974 meeting.

any clarity what they must do about it. For example, if they must accept some change in living standards and lifestyles — which seems unavoidable — then decisions as to how and how much must be taken soon and in an equitable and orderly way, or they will impose themselves later at incalculable economic and political cost.

We are not pessimistic concerning the long-term future. While growth of energy consumption should not and indeed cannot continue at the rate attained in the past two decades, and economic growth is bound to slow down as a consequence, we do not regard an end to economic growth as either desirable or inevitable. But we do foresee a transitional period of extraordinary difficulty and adjustment, until such time as our societies can count on more secure and more abundant energy. The main emphasis of our report, with no intent to slight the importance of energy policy itself, is on the political, social and international consequences of this situation.

We pose some blunt questions. Do governments have the political will to face the truth and to act, and if so, will their peoples give them the power to act? Will they have the strength to avoid unilateral and nationalistic action and to work together for common interests? It will be a test both of democratic institutions and of international solidarity.

I. Dimensions of the Problem

A. THE TIME DIMENSION

Three different time periods should be considered. All three have already begun.

The first period is the present and near future. The consuming countries must cope with the threat to financial and economic health and stability caused principally by the sudden rise in the price of oil. They also face a potential crisis of supply if the Middle East peace negotiations do not succeed and major oil-producing countries again resort to the "oil weapon" for political reasons. Even without war, those producers, as long as they have an effective cartel, can further limit production as a means of maintaining or increasing prices. Consumers and producers must somehow cooperate to cope with this worsening situation, or they will drift toward mutual antagonism and conflict.

The second period covers the next decade, until 1985, in which the consuming countries, in addition to meeting the continuing financial problem, must make a serious and necessarily costly effort to free themselves from critical dependence on imported oil. This can only be a gradual process, but it will not take place at all unless goals for reduced growth in demand and for development of alternative sources are set now and the necessary decisions are taken in time.

The third period is the longer term, to the end of this century, in which the need is for the timely development of new sources of energy, not only to replace oil imports but to cope with the decline of the world's reserves of hydrocarbon fuels. Here again, governments will have to take decisions in the near future, especially on research and development.

B. EMERGENCE OF A POWERFUL NEW ACTOR

Recent developments have wrought significant changes in the international order, especially in overall relationships between industrial and raw-material-producing countries. The existence of the oil cartel, with its power to fix prices, introduces a fourth party, and a very powerful one indeed, into relations among the Trilateral regions, whose economies are affected in different ways. The power of the Organization of Petroleum Exporting Countries (OPEC) is felt particularly by Western Europe and Japan, which cannot dispense with oil imports from the Middle East. The United States remains the most powerful economy, but its freedom of maneuver has been hampered by the weakening of its European and Japanese partners and by its inability to limit the rise in the price of oil.

C. THE IMPACT OF HIGH OIL PRICES

In order to keep their economies going, the consuming countries have paid the high prices set by OPEC. Some of them are already in a serious financial plight because of large deficits in their balance of trade, the drain on their financial reserves, and the decline of their capacity to borrow. The positions of Italy, Great Britain, and France are critical.

What happens when an oil-importing country cannot borrow further? It can set up quantitative restrictions on trade, or let its currency depreciate, or sell its reserves, or become bankrupt and come to terms with its creditors. At some point the principal creditors (probably the United States, Germany, and the producing countries) will have to discuss with the debtors what is to be done.

The entire group of consuming countries, moreover, must deal with the question of "recycling" the oil payment money not balanced by exports to the producers. The sums, which have been conservatively estimated at $60 billion for 1974 alone and up to $650 billion (World Bank estimate) for the period to 1980, are or will be too large for the private banking system to handle without backing by central banks or governments. The process of investment in the industrial countries goes on, as individual oil-producing states put their funds on deposit, make their own decisions on short or long-term investment, or conclude bilateral agreements with consuming states. But the oil money is piling up too quickly, there is insufficient time for adjustment, and the funds do not go back to the consuming states which need them the most. And recycling is not a permanent solution.

The problem of mounting debts which cannot be repaid is of great urgency and may become unmanageable. Appeals to the producing states to relieve the situation by reducing the price of oil, whether based on political sympathy, common interest in a viable world economy, or the dangers of confrontation, have not induced them to do so. As demand is cut by conservation, they are in a position to reduce the supply and maintain income by raising the price still higher. Should they henceforward, as it is intimated, index the price of oil on the rate of inflation in the consuming countries, this will increase further the inflationary effect of the whole process.

The less-developed countries which have little or no oil and must now pay high prices for energy and other essential imports are in a desperate situation from which they cannot escape by themselves. They will have a steadily increasing burden of indebtedness which they cannot reduce substantially by conservation or import substitution. They do

128

not have the resources in technology and infrastructure to adapt their economies to the new situation. Both the advanced industrial countries and the oil-producing countries will have to help, through concessional aid and other means.*

D. THE MIDDLE EAST SITUATION

Political conflicts in the Middle East, especially the Arab-Israeli conflict, add to the critical nature of the problem. Progress toward Arab-Israeli peace settlements has been slow or non-existent since the conclusion of the interim cease-fire and separation-of-forces agreements following the Yom Kippur war. Each side is building up its armed strength. Israel fears for its existence (which is openly rejected by radical Arab elements) and suspects that compromise agreements would only be the prelude to new Arab claims. The Arabs, especially since the summit meeting at Rabat, have taken positions which make negotiation with Israel more difficult. A new war is a strong possibility. If governments do not take timely decisions now, they may be forced to take them under crisis conditions which will greatly limit their choices.

In a number of contingencies, the Arab states might act to cut down or cut off oil exports to Western countries: in case of a resumption of war with Israel, certainly; in case of failure to reach a settlement within a relatively short time, probably; to prevent the extension of Western loans to Israel or the conclusion by the E.E.C. of a trade agreement with Israel, possibly. A substantial reduction in oil supply would, of course, increase the risk of economic collapse of the more vulnerable consuming countries.

In the absence of an understanding with the Soviet Union covering the dangerous contingencies in the Middle East, that country, which has given strong political and material support to the Arabs against Israel, may create further serious problems for the Western nations in maintaining their security and vital economic interests.

E. INTRA-EUROPEAN RELATIONS

The oil crisis has added to the predicament of a European Community already suffering from serious trade and monetary imbalances. The result has been to deprive the Community of its policy potential not only in regard to energy but also in other major fields. Inflation has increased

---

*The Trilateral Task Force on Relations with Developing Countries has submitted two reports which deal with this matter. The first (June 1974) is entitled *A Turning Point in North-South Economic Relations;* the second (December 1974) is called *OPEC, the Trilateral World and the Developing Countries: New Arrangements for Cooperation, 1976-1980.*

to a point where it endangers political stability in individual countries, and the differential between rates of inflation drives the members of the Community further apart. As long as the balances of payments of E.E.C. member states are diversely affected by the rise in the price of oil, no progress can be made toward a common monetary policy.

As each member of the Community is hit by the effects of high oil prices, its natural reaction has been to take national measures to protect its own economy, sometimes to the detriment of others, and to look for help to individual governments rather than through a joint approach. Only recently has there been a growing awareness of the serious implications of the financial crisis and of the need for a common loan fund.

Furthermore, the continued emphasis on making decisions through intergovernmental mechanisms rather than through the Community institutions has made it impossible for the Community either to respond quickly to an emergency or to adopt long-term policies which are more than non-committal pledges. The uncertainty over Britain's participation adds to the near-paralysis of the Community institutions.

Less tangible but nonetheless real are the effects on mutual trust of the lack of solidarity shown by the European countries when the Arab states in 1973 cut back oil exports and raised prices. The Community institutions were not effective. Individual members, seeing recurrent use of the oil weapon as the most real danger, did not resist the temptation to seek reinsurance through bilateral deals with oil-producing countries at the risk of overbidding and of eroding the common commercial policy.

The absence of a common energy policy for the E.E.C. made it difficult to face the crisis together at its outbreak. The divisive effects of having to make choices between the Arabs and the Americans, in turn, have hampered the creation of a comprehensive European energy policy. Without such a policy, Europe can hardly play a strong and constructive role together with North America and Japan in dealing with the energy problem either in the near future or over the long term.

F. EUROPEAN-AMERICAN RELATIONS

When the impact of the Middle East war, the Arab oil embargo and the cutback in production struck the Western world, it revealed an apparent conflict of vital interests between Europe and the United States. During the October war the United States concentrated on issues of military and political security and underestimated the difficulties of the Europeans, whereas Europe thought of economic security first and underestimated the involvement of the Soviet Union. In the period following the war these differences were smoothed over as the two sides began talks on energy matters and tried to improve the procedures for consultation within their alliance. Nevertheless, the potential conflict of interests remains and could come to the surface if the Middle East again erupts in war or if the financial strain bears too heavily on Europe. It is rooted in the profound difference in vulnerability between Europe and the United States, which recent events have widened. The United States has become relatively stronger, owing to the abundance of its energy resources and a strong economic position which should attract the surplus funds of the oil-producing states. Europe is militarily dependent on America and economically dependent on the oil-producing states of the Middle East. Both types of dependence will endure for some time and have to be kept in balance.

The functioning of the Atlantic Alliance is inescapably affected by these developments. Besides bringing to the fore differences of outlook on the Middle East, they may weaken the defense of Western Europe itself. The cost of oil imports will probably induce the European states to reduce their military expenditures at a time when the U.S. Congress is considering the reduction of American forces stationed in Europe. This double trend will have a destabilizing effect on security in Europe, which in turn will weaken the security of all members of the alliance, including the United States.

The gap in strength between America and Europe, which energy factors have increased, thus creates problems which cannot be easily solved within the alliance as it now functions. Both parties have an interest in making it more effective in consideration of problems and adoption of consistent policies outside of Europe, particularly in the Middle East. It is important to the alliance as a whole that the European countries improve their economic position with oil-producing states, and also that a common approach be found to the political issues involving those states, especially to the question of a settlement between Israel and its Arab neighbors.

G. JAPANESE-AMERICAN RELATIONS

Japan's dependence on Middle East oil, even greater than Europe's, dictated a similar attitude toward the October war and led to public statements of policy sympathetic to Arab views on terms of political settlement with Israel. Japan's statements and policies, however, did not create differences with the United States comparable to the controversies and recriminations which marked European-American relations, for Japan was remote both geographically and politically from the Middle East conflict. Nevertheless, Japan's scramble for oil in the world market and its intensified efforts to secure future supplies through direct deals with producing countries in the wake of the crisis caused considerable apprehension on the part of the United States, which was trying to bring about a common front of consumers and an approach based on non-discriminatory access. Subsequent developments, however, have shown that Japan's achievement in direct deals was relatively small.

Such strains as these Japanese activities caused were largely dissipated by Japan's participation in the Washington conference on energy in February 1974 and in the work of the Energy Coordinating Group. But there remain fundamental differences in the positions of the two nations, one with vast reserves of potential energy and the other with virtually none. Japan's support for international efforts for closer co-operation among consuming countries carries the proviso that they will not lead to confrontation with producing countries, for of all the developed countries Japan is the most vulnerable, economically and politically, to interruption of oil supplies. Japan's continued dependence on imported oil, and on Middle East oil in particular, requires it to keep on good terms with producing states, to diversify its sources of energy, and to draw upon the resources of North America.

These factors carry the danger of conflicting Japanese and American policies in the future, especially if the Arab states should again use oil as a political weapon. The sensitivity of both nations to their trade relations may increase the potential for disharmony and dispute if world economic conditions deteriorate. Closer and more frequent consultation, both official and non-governmental, will be needed to prevent friction and conflicts of interest between the two countries.

II. The Response to the Problem

The following, in brief summary, is the record of action, national and international, in response to the energy crisis.

A. NORTH AMERICA
In the United States the Middle East war, the Arab oil embargo, and the threat to the security of future supply prompted emergency measures to cope with immediate shortages, a cut in demand in response to conservation recommendations and higher prices, and the launching of "Project Independence," with the aim of ensuring a stable supply and eliminating dependence on foreign sources by 1980. The Executive and the Congress failed to agree on a number of aspects of energy policy, however, and no comprehensive long-term plan was adopted. Certain specific governmental actions have been taken, through legislation or executive decision, (a) to encourage economy of use, (b) to promote the expansion of domestic oil and gas production, (c) to authorize and expedite building of the Alaska pipeline, (d) to set terms for increased mining of coal, (e) to accelerate production of nuclear power, and (f) to make available increased funds for research and development of solar, geothermal and other forms of energy.

These are largely ad hoc measures and half-measures which by themselves do not constitute a comprehensive policy and have not brought decisive results. The ending of the Arab embargo and the easing of the supply situation in the spring of 1974 lessened the sense of urgency. By autumn, consumption of oil was slightly below the level of the same time the year before (reflecting definite progress in conservation), and dependence on imports (a little over one-third of total oil consumption) remained unchanged. Domestic oil production has continued to decline, and although the oil and gas industry has decided to invest large sums in exploration and production, those investments will not show results for several years. The government's plan for Project Independence, finally presented to the public in November 1974, at least set an agenda for debate on policy.

Secretary Kissinger on November 14, in the context of proposals for comprehensive agreements and cooperation among the consuming countries on many aspects of energy policy, outlined an American policy of drastic conservation and development of new sources, with a goal of reducing oil imports in the next decade to a level of one million barrels per day. Much of the American program will require further policy decisions and legislation before going into effect.

Canada did not have to respond with drastic measures to the energy crisis, and it would be politically difficult to do so as long as large exports of oil and gas still go to the United States. It had some shortage in its eastern provinces which are dependent on imported oil, even though the country is a net exporter. Eventual completion of the pipeline from the Alberta oil fields to Montreal should give Canada the capability for self-sufficiency, if it should so choose, but rising nationwide demand and prospective declining production from existing oil and gas fields raise questions for the next decade unless new sources are developed. Possessed of large potential energy resources in the Athabasca tar sands and possibly in Arctic oil and gas, Canada has adopted a policy of developing its energy at a rate suited to its own needs and not primarily for export.

Engaged in the search for a national energy policy, Canada has rejected the idea of a "continental" energy program with the United States. However, the relationship of the two nations in energy, as in other fields, remains a unique and complex one. Export of Canadian oil and gas to the United States will probably continue for some years, although at a declining rate unless and until new sources surplus to Canada's needs are developed.

B. WESTERN EUROPE

Because the E.E.C. has not succeeded in the attempt to establish a common energy policy, the Europeans have responded to the present crisis primarily on a national basis. The response was therefore diverse, and it was limited. Only the Netherlands embarked on a drastic, long-term program to save energy, achieving substantial results through a combination of government initiative and the response of the population and of private industry. Italy, despite its financial plight, has a poor record on conservation. France, after a year in which reduction of demand in real terms was negligible, has set a financial ceiling for oil imports in 1975 and taken measures to restrict consumption. Britain, which has done little to reduce consumption other than to let higher prices take their toll, is relying heavily on future oil and gas from the North Sea (and already mortgaging it) and on increased use of coal. Germany, like Britain, has raised coal production targets modestly. Both France and Germany are committed to a substantial growth in the production of nuclear energy.

The European Commission has recommended a broad and ambitious program of conservation and development of energy over the next decade, with emphasis on nuclear energy and gas. But the program has not been accepted by governments. Meanwhile, the member countries go their respective ways. The financial resources they have devoted to exploration and to technology in order to reduce dependence on imports do not compare, even in relative terms, with the efforts deployed in the United States. Nor have European governments begun to face hard choices such as those Japan is already taking for the adaptation and restructuring of industry.

C. JAPAN

The oil crisis triggered by the October war had an immediate and severe impact on the Japanese economy, including further acceleration of an already high rate of inflation. The government's response was slow, confused, and ineffective. Its frantic pursuit of available oil earned considerable criticism in other consuming countries. Not until near the end of 1973 did the government introduce mandatory measures cutting oil and electricity consumption (by 10 and later by 15 percent in the industrial sector) and impose price controls on petroleum products and other commodities. When the oil supply situation improved, it abolished the mandatory conservation measures and lifted price controls except on a few essential commodities. Higher prices and economic slowdown have worked to constrain oil consumption, which is estimated at 3 to 4 percent less in 1974 than in 1973, with imports of oil slightly (2 to 3 percent) less than the 1973 level of 5.2 million barrels per day.

The Japanese government has promised for the spring of 1975 a comprehensive energy policy, with projections of the nation's demand-supply situation in 1980 and 1985. According to the preliminary report, average annual growth of primary energy supply from 1973 to 1985 is estimated at 5.7 percent (as against 11.7 percent for 1962-1972). But imported energy is still estimated to account for 82.3 percent of total primary energy supply in 1985, compared with 86.4 percent in 1972. Oil imports would grow at an annual rate of 3.8 percent, about one-fourth the actual growth rate in the five years to 1973.

In order to reduce excessive dependence on imported energy, Japan is planning intensified development of its limited indigenous energy resources, development of nuclear power, and a long-term research and development program (aimed at the year 2000) on solar energy, geothermal energy, coal gasification, and other new sources. All this can make a difference, but there is no chance of a substantial reduction in dependence on imported energy and oil in particular.

In view of the limited energy supply and higher cost, Japan envisages further economy in energy consumption and slower economic growth. It accepts the necessity, in order to maintain a viable economy and social stability, of efforts to shift the economic structure from energy-intensive industries to those which are intensive in knowledge and technology. This structural change is a long-term solution for the energy problem, requiring reallocation of resources, labor, and investment.

D. INTERNATIONAL ACTION

No agreed international action was taken in the latter months of 1973 to meet the embargo and production cuts decided by the Arab states or the price rises determined by OPEC. Indeed, the differing reactions by the United States, Japan, and the E.E.C. (and among members of the E.E.C.) illustrated a general view that each could serve its interests better through separate action. The first serious attempt to establish common approaches was the Washington conference of thirteen nations in February 1974. The Energy Coordinating Group, which grew out of that conference, has been working out cooperative programs covering conservation and restraint of demand, development of new sources, emergency sharing, research and development, financial aspects, the possibility of meetings of consuming and producing countries, and the role of the international oil companies.

This work proceeded at a disappointingly slow pace but finally produced an emergency oil-sharing plan and a new International Energy Agency, which came into being in November 1974. The agreement on sharing, which will be activated automatically when restriction of supply reaches a given point, is a major achievement helping to blunt the damaging effects of embargoes or cutbacks. The new agency, embracing all the Trilateral countries except for France and Norway and with a procedure of weighted voting likely to produce decisions, should be stronger than the E.E.C. or the O.E.C.D. and should play an important role as a policy-making and operational body. The real test, however, will be on the policies to be adopted rather than the institutions and the procedures through which they may be reached.

On the pressing financial question, international action has been limited to bilateral loans to ease the plight of countries in serious trouble (e.g., a large German loan to Italy), and to the establishment by the International Monetary Fund of an "oil facility" for loans to countries hit hardest by higher oil prices, mainly the poorest of the less-developed countries. These arrangements provide for only a few billion dollars of loan money, whereas the deficits will be many times that. As Italy is followed by other consuming countries in reaching the limits of their

136

borrowing capacity, with no drop in what they must pay for oil, the need for timely effective international measures to prevent the worst and to avoid a wave of destructive nationalistic actions and counteractions should be apparent. Belatedly, as illustrated by Secretary Kissinger's proposal of a fund starting with $25 billion for use in 1975, governments have realized the need for the availability of large common funds which can be used flexibly and linked to agreed policies and goals in the energy field.

However one looks at this record of response to the energy crisis, some conclusions are obvious. It has been halting, piecemeal, often inconsistent, and inadequate. Where drastic action is called for, it has not been taken. The governments have been timid. The general public has followed a philosophy of business as usual and hope for the best. Meanwhile, the financial crisis has grown, political dangers have increased, and international action is postponed.

III.   THE NEED FOR NEW APPROACHES:
A LONG-TERM STRATEGY

*In the light of this record we reaffirm the main recom-
mendations of the earlier report of this Task Force (June
1974): the need for a joint commitment by the Trilateral
countries to the efficient use and rational development
of energy (meeting its high cost as may be necessary)
with a general strategy and plan covering the next twenty
years; and the requirement for early action, national and
international, toward fulfillment of that commitment.*

The common plan should establish a series of goals respecting levels of
energy consumption, efforts for economy of use, rates of development,
reduction of dependence on energy imported from outside the Trilateral
area, and meeting the high cost of essential energy whether imported or
produced at home. Obviously it is not wise or desirable to provide precise sets of figures to illustrate recommendations for a strategy which
looks a decade and more ahead. But in the belief that some general
targets for the next ten years should be established as a spur to necessary national and international action, we make the following recommendations.

A.   GROWTH AND LEVEL OF DEMAND

*The annual rate of increase in energy consumption over
the next decade should be held below 2 percent in North
America, 3 percent in Western Europe, and 4 percent
in Japan.*

This will mean a drastic reduction of demand but should still permit
a modest rate of economic growth. The lower figure should be possible
for the United States (which would still have the highest per capita
consumption), and the higher figure for Japan (which would have the
lowest per capita consumption), with Europe in between. These rates
may be compared with those existing before 1973 (which then were
expected to continue) of roughly 4.5 percent for the U.S., 5.5 percent
for Europe, and 11.7 percent for Japan.

The fictional nature of projections based on those earlier rates
makes it somewhat unreal to state the "savings" which can be realized
by conservation, but holding demand to a 2 percent annual increase in
the United States, for example, would mean that by 1985 consumption

would be running 27 percent less than originally projected. Savings in Europe and in Japan, with higher rates of pre-crisis projection, would be correspondingly greater.

TABLE 1. ENERGY CONSUMPTION IN TRILATERAL AREAS
(in millions of metric tons of coal equivalent)

Area	1972 (actual)	1975	1980	1985
United States	2425	2573	2841	3137
		(projected at 2% annual increase)		
Canada	235	249	275	304
		(projected at 2% annual increase)		
European Community	1180	1290	1495	1734
		(projected at 3% annual increase)		
Japan	345	388	472	574
		(projected at 4% annual increase)		

Source: Adapted from 1973 *United Nations Statistical Yearbook,* pp. 348-50.

B. EFFICIENCY OF USE

To hold demand growth at the proposed levels will require a major successful effort to reduce waste and increase efficiency of use. Our societies should be ever alert to the possibilities of even larger reductions in consumption, bringing demand closer to or below the level of annual renewal rather than of increase.

The first requirement is a psychological change: acceptance of the fact that the era of cheap and abundant energy is over and a positive willingness to adjust to it. The second requirement is action on a number of fronts.

In the case of industrial consumption the price mechanism should be the main incentive to saving energy. Some measures can be taken at once, without heavy investment. In other cases longer lead-times or new advances in technology will be required. It should be noted that investment in efficiency of use will often be much less than for a corresponding increase in supply, and the return will often be more rapid.

Public policy will have an essential role in explication and persuasion, in enacting and enforcing standards, in allocating energy to different uses, in equitable distribution of fuels, in helping to plan and finance economic adjustment and change, in reorganizing systems of transport, and in sponsoring research. Governments should aim at avoiding the expansion of energy-intensive industries and services. For instance, they should drastically reduce the building of new airports and the movement of freight by air. Such decisions would be more acceptable if taken as a result of Trilateral agreement. Individual countries, of course, all have their special conditions; Japan, for example, has less margin before cutting into the bone of essential industrial production.

Limitation of civilian consumption will also be necessary. Here a balance will have to be struck between the price mechanism and the use of mandatory controls. (The social and political implications of conservation are considered in Part VI of this report.)

C. DEVELOPMENT OF ADDITIONAL ENERGY

The effort to increase supply within the next few years must rest primarily on intensified production of known reserves of fossil fuels in areas of secure supply.

The first priority should go to the oil and gas resources of the North Sea and Alaska. The other major possibility is coal, which North America, Europe, South Africa and Australia have in quantity. Coal and its derivatives will not only supplement oil but in many instances will provide a substitute for it. Early decisions are necessary to perfect the technology for gasification of coal and extraction of oil from shale and tar sands, although significant energy supplies from the latter two sources may not appear until the mid-1980's. The private oil companies will continue to have a significant role in the development of new sources, especially in investment decisions on exploration and production.

The consuming countries should consult on the estimates each should set for the production of coal, oil, natural gas, nuclear power, hydro power, and oil from shale and tar sands, for 1980 and 1985.

The resultant figures would indicate not only the goals for each country and region but also the picture for the consuming countries as a whole, including the possibilities for trade in energy resources between them. By 1985, each of the Trilateral regions should strive to cover 15 percent of total energy consumption with nuclear power. We recognize that this is an ambitious goal, in view of the continuing problems regarding safety, environmental protection, and possible diversion of nuclear

140

materials, and in view of the understandable public concern on these matters.

> *For the period after 1985 a similar but much more tentative set of goals should be set, with initial emphasis on research and development and continuing flexibility to adjust programs to scientific and technological change.*

Oil shale, tar sands and nuclear power should by then be contributing much more energy. While research on solar energy, geothermal energy, atomic fusion, and other possible sources should be given full rein, our conclusion is that the energy base from 1985 to the end of the century will still rest largely on fossil fuels (increasingly on coal and its derivatives) and on nuclear fission reactors. In planning for the long term, the competent authorities in the Trilateral countries should look continually at the comparative advantages and disadvantages of the various types of energy and try to choose the least disadvantageous combination in making their decisions on development.

D. REDUCTION OF DEPENDENCE ON OUTSIDE ENERGY

> *The United States and Canada should each strive for a position of substantial self-sufficiency in energy by 1985.*

Although they might still be importing some OPEC oil (and the U.S. might be importing oil from Canada), the two countries should aim at holding imports of oil from uncertain sources to a level of less than 5 percent of total primary energy use. They should be, for all practical purposes, free to keep their economies going without disruption in case of a cutoff of OPEC oil; they would then not have to make demands on limited oil supplies available to other consuming countries and could even contribute to the total energy supply if they had built up additional export capacity in coal and other fuels.

> *The E.E.C. should reduce its dependence on uncertain imports of oil and gas, from the present 60 percent to 40 percent by 1985. In the same period, Japan should correspondingly reduce its dependence from 75 percent to 65 percent.*

We recognize that neither Western Europe as a whole nor Japan can achieve energy independence for many years. The need is for immediate decisions proving a serious intent to move in that direction, for some noticeable progress within a few years, and for commitment to specific goals and time schedules. Further lowering of the above percentages for Europe and Japan should be envisaged after 1985, especially through the growth of nuclear energy, but the setting of specific goals can await intervening developments.

We do not regard possible imports of oil and gas from non-OPEC sources as likely to change the basic problem. Prospects exist for increased production and new discoveries in or offshore Asia, Africa and Latin America, but since any country so favored would probably soon join OPEC, security of supply is uncertain. All possibilities, however, should be seriously explored. As to other fuels, the potential for coal supplies from Australia and South Africa is high.

The Soviet Union has vast reserves of energy, but its own increasing demands will limit its capacity to export. While some Soviet fuels should be available for Europe and Japan, the grandiose proposals under discussion by U.S. and Japanese companies with the Soviet government for the development and export of oil and gas seem to involve high costs and high risks, and should be weighed against comparable investments elsewhere. It is natural for Japan to diversify its sources of energy by looking to China (from which its oil imports are increasing) and to the U.S.S.R. It is doubtful whether Japan or any of the consuming countries could meet more than a small percentage (say 5 percent) of its total energy demand from Communist countries, and it would not be wise from a political standpoint to incur any substantial degree of dependence on them. But these risks are no greater than those of present dependence on the Middle East, and to diversify sources of energy means to diversify political risks.

E. EMERGENCY SHARING

We stress the importance of agreement on stockpiling and on sharing energy supplies in an emergency, and hope that all the Trilateral governments will accept the plan of the Energy Coordinating Group.

A strong and workable plan for coping with a cutoff of oil imports or other serious energy shortages is essential, not least for the deterrent effect in preventing such an emergency. We believe France and Norway would find it in their interest and in the common interest to join the emergency plan to maintain solidarity with the others in the event of crisis.

It is essential that the provisions for sharing be linked to equitable standards for conservation; otherwise, the provident will merely be subsidizing the improvident. The international oil companies should

142

cooperate in making the emergency plan work and should make all the necessary information on reserves, supplies, and prices available to the participating governments.

F. COOPERATION IN RESEARCH

Taking account of all the requirements of the long-term energy plan, the United States, Canada, the E.E.C. and Japan should work out a general framework for cooperation in energy research and development, within which the necessary specific arrangements can be made.

The Trilateral countries cannot afford separate and competing efforts in this field. On conservation, on many aspects of the development of nuclear energy, and on experimentation with new and still unusable forms of energy, they must put science and technology to work where there are the best chances for achieving results.

G. THE FINANCIAL BURDEN

Financial problems will beset the consuming countries at every stage of their long-term strategy, as they will be paying for high-cost energy whether it comes from OPEC sources or from their own. But the most serious stage, as indicated earlier, is the immediate one: now and the next few years when huge sums of money in payment for oil are being transferred to the account of producing countries. We shall not, in this report, make specific recommendations on such matters as emergency credits, arrangements between governments and private banks, types and directions of investment for oil money, or the role of the international financial institutions. We wish to stress three more general points:

1. *The financially stronger countries, frankly recognizing common political interests, should be prepared to help their partners whose economies have been thrown into crisis by the effects of the high price of oil.* This aid should be conditioned upon the most rigorous measures of self-discipline and self-help on the part of the recipients (although not with rigid uniform standards) and accompanied by joint commitments to preserve the international trading and financial system. All should recognize that emergency loans do not provide a lasting solution, and that the financially stronger countries such as the United States and Germany cannot assume the mounting burden of debt of the others.

2. *The consuming countries must maintain continuing contact and negotiation with the producing countries to deal with the question*

of oil price in the context of the many other questions, both economic and political, in which both sides are interested. A confrontation on the isolated issue of oil price should be avoided. But the producing countries must recognize the crucial importance of that issue to the future of the world economy. Discussion with them is necessary at an early date on the basis of cooperation.

3. *The consuming countries must begin at once to put themselves in a position where they are less dependent on imported oil.* This is necessary both to reduce the drain on their financial reserves and to give them greater bargaining power for lower oil prices. Thus, for the price problem as for the supply problem, the need is for concerted and far-reaching action to conserve energy and to develop alternatives to imported oil.

H. AVOIDANCE OF NATIONALISTIC MEASURES

The consuming countries should avoid attempting to solve problems which derive from the energy crisis with nationalistic measures such as devaluation of currencies and new controls on imports or exports.

Such measures, which would only lead to a spiral of competitive actions, could gravely damage the trading and financial system and the interests of all concerned. On investments in energy the consuming countries should have an agreed policy so as to avoid duplication at a time when the need for capital will far exceed the availability of funds.

IV. Relations with Oil-Producing Countries

Among the political challenges posed to the Trilateral countries by the energy problem, the foremost is to relations among themselves. But another challenge demands their immediate attention, that of relations with the oil-exporting countries, especially those in the Middle East. How is the adjustment to be made between vital consumer interests and the exercise by the producers of their new "oil power"?

In narrow terms, the main problem is one of persuasion: how to convince the members of OPEC to keep up the supply of oil, at bearable prices, during the period of continuing dependence. One method is diplomatic argument, which by itself is not likely to prevail against counter-argument based on tangible interest. Another method is economic pressure. No one consuming country, however, has the capacity to exert decisive pressure on the producers, and while consumer solidarity is useful and even necessary as a means of balancing the solidarity of the members of OPEC, attempts to mobilize collective economic pressure on them are of limited effectiveness because the preponderance of bargaining power is on their side. Economic warfare, in the form of attempts to deny food or other supplies, will court political disaster without bringing the desired results. Military action must be ruled out.

These and other considerations argue for a broader and more positive approach, seeking common and reciprocal interests going far beyond oil which can be furthered by cooperation in a variety of forms, bilateral and multilateral. The ensuing paragraphs touch on these interests and opportunities. While some of them apply to all members of OPEC, most of them are particularly applicable to the producing countries of the Middle East, for they are at the heart of the problem.

A. THE ARAB-ISRAELI CONFLICT

The Trilateral countries have to recognize that the question of the supply of oil cannot be separated from the existence of political conflict in the Middle East. The prospect that a new crisis would bring a new reduction or cutoff of Arab oil and again drive the consuming nations apart highlights the need for an early settlement and for an agreed American-European-Japanese approach to it.

This does not mean that the diplomatic roles would not be different; the United States will continue to be more directly and deeply involved than Europe or Japan in the process of mediation and negotiation, and in maintaining a balance with the Soviet Union and seeking its cooperation. The United States, with the Soviet Union, has a special responsibility, for only these two powers have the capacity to act to prevent war or to impose peace. But others who have a strong interest in Arab-Israeli peace may contribute to its achievement. Therefore, the negotiations should not be solely in American hands, with the other consuming countries shut out, nor should the latter take refuge in statements of policy publicly placating the Arabs which make more difficult the task of reaching a negotiated settlement. The Europeans and Japanese will feel involved in the policy only if they have a share in the peace negotiations; hence the need for a process of political consultation. All should know the shape of an emerging settlement, especially those which may be involved in guaranteeing it. In fact, American, European and Japanese ideas on the general terms of settlement, based essentially on the principle of non-acquisition of territory by force and the right of all states to secure existence, are not widely different. All have an interest, too, in timely negotiations, for all will suffer from the consequences of the indefinite deferral of a settlement. An agreed approach, allowing wide scope for changing tactics and for the parties themselves to come together on the final terms, should increase the chances both of Middle East peace and of continued access to oil. If the peoples of our countries can see the clear connection between the question of an Arab-Israeli settlement, that of energy, and that of international security and stability, they are more likely to support the related policies which are needed to deal with these questions.

B. COMMON INTERESTS IN SECURITY

The rivalries of local states and of outside powers have made the Middle East a region of dangerous instability. Members of the Trilateral group of nations, in different ways, can contribute to the security of the region. Certain of the major oil-producing states regard it as important that the existing balance not be upset and that no outside power acquire predominant power in the area of the Persian (Arabian) Gulf. Some of the governing regimes have uncertain or unfriendly relations with other states of the region, or must deal with unstable internal situations. Their newly-acquired wealth may serve as an invitation to subversion, revolution, or intervention from outside. Presumably they have a stake in the avoidance of strife and may see a benefit to their security in the assurance of Western interest and in the presence of Western forces in the area, so long as the latter serve not as a threat of intervention in conflicts of local states but as support for their independence and nonalignment.

Similarly, their acquisition of American or European arms for the fulfillment of plans for national defense, besides helping to reduce balance-of-payments deficits from oil sales, opens doors to broad cooperation in military and technological fields. The obvious political and economic advantages of such sales, however, should not obscure the dangers of providing ever more sophisticated weapons, stimulating arms races or encouraging militarism. The danger of the spread of nuclear weapons to the region cannot be overlooked. The supply of arms is a complex matter, to which supplying and receiving countries should address themselves in a framework of common interest in security. We recommend, on the side of the suppliers, the establishment of some mechanism, possibly in the framework of the Atlantic Alliance, so that they may consult, exchange information, establish limits of competition, and coordinate decisions, bearing in mind the desirability of eventual negotiation, including the Soviet Union, for a general agreement on arms deliveries and arms levels.

C. NATIONAL DEVELOPMENT PROGRAMS

The highest priority in economic cooperation goes to helping the producing countries carry out their programs for the improvement of agriculture and the growth of basic industries. Besides meeting their wants, rapid development will promote exports of the industrialized countries and cut down the oil money balances. The countries of the Middle East and North Africa, on their part, should see the need for coordinating their development programs so as to avoid the building up of surplus capacities in their new industries over the next few years.

The building of petroleum-related industries such as refining and petrochemicals in the producing countries is natural and inevitable. The consuming countries should provide help, even though the temporary effect will be to add to OPEC's bargaining power, create competition for their own industries, and aggravate their situation regarding the cost and supply of oil products.

Similar considerations apply to further exploration for oil and gas in the producing countries. The effort required for it might better be used to develop energy in the consuming countries themselves. But if a basic purpose is to create a many-sided structure of cooperation with the producers, this side can hardly be omitted. It is obviously related to the

147

willingness of the producing countries to continue to supply oil from existing wells.

The producing countries, even those with the largest reserves, are acutely aware that their oil is not inexhaustible. The industrialized countries can help them to prepare for the day when they will look to other sources. Nuclear projects for desalination and generation of industrial power (with effective safeguards against diversion of nuclear material to military use) and joint experiments in solar energy would serve this aim.

D. NEGOTIATIONS ON THE SUPPLY AND PRICE OF OIL

Leaders of consuming countries have appealed directly for the lowering of prices, and leaders of some producing countries, notably Iran, have stated publicly why they do not do so, linking the question to inflation of currencies and the prices of other goods. This is a subject on which governments should talk seriously in private rather than polemically in public. It is, moreover, important to get the cooperation of some of the OPEC governments in sharing the burdens and risks of the recycling process and in making concessionary arrangements for the more needy oil-importing countries.

There are obvious limits on how far trade and prices should or can be handled on a government-to-government basis. But OPEC is not an ordinary phenomenon, the price of oil threatens the industrialized world with possible disaster, and there has to be a basis for discussion which the rulers of the major producing states accept. If talks covering the price of food, fertilizer, and other commodities can lead to greater understanding of difficulties on both sides and open the possibility of a better situation in respect of the supply and the price of oil, then they are well worth undertaking. The price of oil should not be a fixed datum, the central point of a continuing test of bargaining strength, but a derivative of many conditions, economic and political, which make up a long-term, mutually beneficial relationship.

E. INVESTMENT OF OIL MONEY OUTSIDE THE PRODUCING COUNTRIES

A wide field for cooperation exists in decisions on the investment of the oil producers' surplus funds in the consuming countries. This side of the economic relationship provides for the first time a counterpart to the more familiar one of the flow of investment in the other direction. It creates mutuality, with each side having an interest in an inflow of resources for development and a concern for retaining control of fundamental economic decisions. In addition to profitable investment, the oil-producing states presumably have an interest in helping the consuming states to avoid serious economic dislocation or collapse under the burden of payments for oil, which could disrupt their own economies as well and strain political relations more than they wish.

The investment of producing countries' surplus oil funds in the development of energy in the developed countries is a special case, for it raises the question whether they will wish to contribute to the possible erosion of prices and of the bargaining position they now enjoy. They may find that it is in their interest to do so, since oil will always be a premium fuel and the development of energy elsewhere will tend to make their own reserves last longer. Involvement in this type of undertaking could help create in oil-producing and industrialized countries alike a habit of looking together at the total energy situation in the long term and as a world problem.

The ability of the industrial countries to provide development capital for the less-developed and energy-poor countries of the Third World will be reduced because of the outflow of funds to pay for imported oil and the need for large amounts of capital to develop new sources of energy. The capacity of the oil-producing countries to furnish such capital, in contrast, will be greatly increased. They will have the opportunity, using existing international institutions or new ones of their own, to make investments which could give a strong impetus to the economic development of the Third World.

F. A LARGER ROLE IN WORLD AFFAIRS

The oil-producing countries do not play a role in international consultations and decisions relating to the world economy commensurate with their now greatly increased wealth and power. For example, they now hold about 5 percent of the voting power in the World Bank and the I.M.F. The industrialized countries should encourage their increasing participation, both in existing and future international institutions and in informal associations, in dealing with the familiar questions of finance, trade, and development. This will mean giving them more voting strength and top-level appointments, and larger responsibilities as well, with a corresponding reduction of the role of others. With the growing urgency of problems such as the balance of food and population, the effects of technological change, and protection of the world environment, the consuming and producing countries can cultivate responsible common interest in the exploration of possible responses and the building of new international institutions.

G. SPECIAL RELATIONSHIPS

Another influence which may modify the picture of confrontation over oil between consuming and producing countries is the variety of political interests, cultural ties and other factors which differentiate individual members of one group from each other and strengthen relationships with countries on the other side. Thus, the fact that a European nation or the United States may have a close association with a particular producing country is both natural and generally useful, so long as it does not weaken the position of the Trilateral countries as a whole. If OPEC or the Arab bloc loses cohesion, it will be because the members are following their own interests as they see them, rather than because of outside pressure or manipulation. The Middle East, in particular, is a region of many conflicting local interests, and oil solidarity has not displaced all of them.

There should be no hard and fast rules on how to approach the oil-producing countries either on oil matters alone or on the broader possibilities of cooperation. The private international oil companies are no longer in a position where they can make decisions or negotiate effectively with producing states concerning levels of production or the price of oil. Deprived of their assets in the producing countries (loss of the remaining equity being only a matter of time), they may be less subject to producer pressure and better able to serve the interests of the consuming countries. But the governments of the latter will be more directly involved with the producing countries than in the past.

The approach should be one of cooperation, not confrontation, but with a generally agreed strategy which takes account of differing positions of individual consuming countries. Of course, it takes two sides to produce cooperation, only one to produce confrontation. The important objective, in our view, is a serious and productive negotiation with the producing countries looking toward long-term solutions. It is desirable neither to rush into this without an agreed approach and strategy nor to delay unduly while seeking total congruence of the positions of the consumers. The approach should be organized by the International Energy Agency in consultation with France. The negotiation should include, at some stage, countries from those neither developed nor possessed of substantial energy resources of their own.

OPEC has not wished to negotiate with a bloc of all the consumers. In the situation of the past year, in which supplies were uncertain, consuming countries have naturally turned to whatever methods appeared to promise some assurance that they would continue to get oil. Some of the bilateral agreements they have made contain specifics on oil deliveries and prices over fixed periods; some specify goods and services to be provided in return; others merely set a general framework of cooperation in many fields. Fortunately, this "scramble" for special arrangements did not do as much harm to general consumer interests as some critics feared, and the benefits to those who made them were often illusory.

There is much to be said for diversity of approach. As long as the general interest in equality of treatment is met and bilateral deals neither push up the price of oil nor unduly restrict the available supply, such arrangements need not be discouraged. When made after consultation and within the bounds of the agreed strategy of consuming states, they may be useful in keeping open doors and raising the total quantity of available oil supplies.

Similarly, the dialogue now begun between the E.E.C. and the Arab League is a promising means of opening up discussion on possible cooperation between European and Arab countries. Although there is no authority on the Arab side which could make a general agreement, the Community could open up the possibility of special arrangements with individual Arab countries. The United States, Canada, and Japan have no reason to object to such discussions or the agreements which emerge from them, again with the proviso that they are in accord with an agreed general strategy and do not damage the interests of others.

As a stimulus or as a supplement to general talks between governments of consuming and producing countries, we suggest that the Trilateral Commission set up an expert group which could discuss unofficially with OPEC representatives a whole gamut of issues (such as energy, trade, monetary matters, and relations with poor developing countries) on which the two groups have both conflicting interests and opportunities for cooperation.

Seizure of such opportunities by both sides could open the way to a large-scale multiplication and flowering of economic and political relationships involving the Trilateral countries with the oil-producing countries. Both should be prepared to share power and to share responsibilities. If the initial period of shock and stress can be surmounted and the process of cooperation can gain momentum, the vexing questions of price, recycling, hot money, and production cuts may be dealt with in the perspective of a growing mutuality of interest.

V. Development of Energy in the Trilateral Region

We have already stressed the need for a common long-term strategy for the development of energy resources in the Trilateral countries themselves. Here we shall look mainly at the international political aspects of such action. They are determined to a large extent by the fact that the resources in question are unevenly distributed. In brief, North America has a strong position in current production and proven reserves of fossil fuels and wide possibilities in offshore and Arctic locations, plus a vast potential for the production of oil from shale and tar sands when the technology for its extraction is further improved; Europe, except for North Sea oil and gas and a declining coal industry, is in a much less favorable position; and Japan has practically no natural fuel resources.

For Europe, North Sea oil and gas present the special problem of the speed of their development. The most rapid possible exploitation would help to reduce dependence on the Middle East. On the other hand, these are depletable resources; Norway is already limiting production for various domestic reasons, and Britain may do the same. We recommend that the policy decisions be taken on a European basis, taking into consideration the total European and Trilateral energy situation and bearing in mind that what Europe can do for itself, particularly in the next decade, will improve its position in regard both to independence of Middle East pressures and to relations with North America on energy sharing and energy development.

If the United States with its Project Independence and Canada with a national energy policy develop their respective resources only to fill their own respective needs, the Europeans and Japanese will surely question the usefulness of international solidarity on other aspects of the energy problem, not to speak of other matters. Nuclear energy cannot promise them substantial relief from heavy dependence on OPEC oil for a long time. They have an obvious interest in the development of North American fossil fuel resources for the purpose of sharing in the increased production.

It may not be easy for the United States and Canada to accept the proposition that their energy reserves should be exploited, and exhausted, more rapidly than they would plan in the light of their own long-term requirements. There is a need for full and frank discussion, within each country and in international discourse, in order to find an agreed balance and reconciliation of possibly conflicting interests. If the solidarity and cooperation of the Trilateral countries is necessary and desirable for reducing dependence on OPEC, for emergency sharing, for coping with high oil prices, and for moving ahead to develop nuclear power and other forms of energy for the future, then it should be valid as well for the development of known resources, whatever their location, within the Trilateral area.

Development of these resources on a large scale will require large new investments, as well as guarantees that the resulting high-cost energy will in fact have an outlet, for instance through long-term purchase contracts. The home countries should welcome added foreign capital, and participating foreign interests would have to share in the risks and in the guarantees.

Governments of the Trilateral countries should try to agree on a set of general rules covering the priority of development of various resources, a common fund to finance and guarantee investments, the degree of domestic and outside participation in investment, estimated volume of production, and the availability of a portion of the product for the export market. Mutually advantageous bilateral arrangements, of course, should not have to await the conclusion of a formal multilateral agreement.

Under appropriate legislation, private and mixed and public companies might all have a role. There is room for wide variety in practice, allowing scope for private enterprise and market forces to do what they can do more efficiently than governments. The wider the area of agreement is, the better the chances are for an overall long-term strategy to work. The sensitivities of Canada or Norway, of Britain or of the United States, are fully understood, and their sovereign governments have the last word, but our countries are not closed national preserves. It is legitimate and desirable, for example, that American companies should participate in the production of North Sea oil, Japanese companies in the mining of American coal, or an E.E.C. consortium in the processing of Canada's tar sands.

This question is of the greatest significance as a test of Trilateral solidarity. Will it be seen as a conflict of national versus foreign interests, or of haves versus have-nots, or as an opportunity for contributions of different kinds to be made by all in the interest of a viable economy for the entire Trilateral region? If our nations do not succeed in finding common ground in dealing with themselves, it is difficult to see how they can stay together in dealing with the oil-producing countries.

VI. Social and Political Change

There can be little doubt that more serious shortages of energy and more drastic adjustment of economic patterns and social lifestyles lie ahead. We have noted that renewal by the Arab states of embargoes and cuts in exports, perhaps more severe than the last time, is a serious possibility, and that the financial drain caused mainly by high oil prices is forcing one consuming country after another to take measures in self-defense. There is nothing to be gained and much to lose if each tries to shift the problems elsewhere, at the expense of other countries and of the international economic system, in order to avoid facing them at home. Finally, the long-term energy strategy recommended by this report as the best course toward a more secure future will make heavy demands on governments, private industry, and the public, particularly in the area of energy conservation. Economic factors will by themselves induce certain changes. But the situation will call for a considerable degree of voluntary cooperation and of acceptance, voluntary or involuntary, of governmental regulation of an increased sector of personal life.

We cannot predict precisely what changes and adjustments will be necessary. The ground rule for civilian consumption should be for the state to ensure a socially just use of energy at the existing price level. This is the condition for the maintenance of a civilized life. Supplementary consumption, whether for heat, lighting, or transport, might be tolerated but at a much higher price.

There will surely be a slower overall growth of the economy, a restructuring of production, a high rate of investment, and a retreat from some of the more extravagant features of our consumer society. The cult of the automobile and the current methods of constructing, heating and cooling buildings can hardly remain unaffected. In essence, there will be a reallocation of capital, labor, technology, and available supplies of energy through the economics of scarcity. We foresee shifts from energy-intensive industries to others which consume less; from relatively non-essential (the highly-developed packaging industry, for example) to more essential production; and from wasteful to energy-efficient methods of transporting people and goods. Such shifts will mean changes in patterns of investment and of employment, a high level of technological unemployment, and perhaps a reduced working week. Serious social strains are bound to appear, especially if the economies of the industrial nations, now exposed to rising costs for energy and for labor, continue to be plagued by inflation and financial instability.

Not all our governments are strong, and it is a virtue of democracy that it is sensitive to the public mood. There are psychological barriers still to be passed in recognition of the challenge. It is a real question, therefore, whether the necessary sacrifices will in fact be accepted by powerful elements in the body politic, be they politicians, civil servants, trade unions, businessmen, or an undefined mass of ordinary citizens. In such cases, there is instability and turmoil whether a government tries to face the crisis or to avoid it. We foresee growing extremism, both of the right and of the left, which will feed on this instability.

Each nation, of course, will have to make its own decisions on how the necessary elements of social discipline, governmental control, and changes in customary modes of living can be reconciled with the vital need to preserve civic freedoms and democratic institutions. But none will be acting in isolation. Political chaos or the coming of anti-democratic forces to power in any of the Trilateral countries would be a most serious danger to their common security.

It is not possible to avert such dangers with vague formulas for solidarity and cooperation. On the economic side, the problems of industrial structure, the environment, and the mobility of labor will call for common planning and for a stronger international system than ever. Politically, sensitivity to each other's problems and agreement on sharing burdens and shortages provide the only way to keep the system from breaking down.

Because all our countries will have to get along with less energy, it is indefensible that they should differ widely in the burdens and the discipline they accept, as they now do on the most important matter of all, conservation. Obviously the standards and practices cannot be the same everywhere, but there should be, first, an acceptance of the principle of equity; second, an attempt to define what is equitable and to get agreement on it; and third, some mechanism, in the International Energy Agency or the O.E.C.D., which could establish general criteria and make judgments on each country's performance.

These social problems, in their consequences as in their causes, are in essence international. Our nations have to attack them together, in the context of the long-term strategy on energy and of common political interests. The steadiness required of governments and the dedication and self-discipline required of the people can hardly be sustained unless the people are convinced that the enterprise is a vital one and that their efforts are being matched by those of their allies. All must have a common sense of purpose, a confidence that democratic methods will see us through, and policies which justify that confidence.

155

All these matters requiring cooperation could be more easily and sensibly handled if the European Community had a common energy policy and could act as a unit in partnership with the United States, Canada, and Japan. Until that degree of unity exists, it is all the more important that all the Western European states, including France and Norway, be in a position to act effectively with other Trilateral countries through such bodies as the International Energy Agency· and the O.E.C.D.

It would be useful to have, in addition, a non-governmental body of experts who could make a long-range evaluation of the social dynamics of the three regions, monitor the evolving situation, and report periodically to governments and to the Secretary-General of the O.E.C.D.

VII.   CONCLUSIONS

Our conclusions have already been given in the body of this report. By way of résumé, we wish to state five broad sets of conclusions while re-emphasizing, under some of them, a number of specific recommendations.

A. A LONG-TERM STRATEGY

The Trilateral countries should have a common long-term strategy covering both the internal and the international aspects of the energy problem.

B. INSTITUTIONS TO MAKE IT WORK

Establishing the strategy and adapting it over time require continuous consultation and negotiation among the Trilateral countries and between them and the oil-producing countries. There must be an effective organizational structure for that purpose, including Trilateral institutions (such as the O.E.C.D. and the International Energy Agency) and an agreed division of labor between such institutions, their member governments, and the European Community.

C. INTERNAL GOALS

To reach a better balance between supply and demand in energy, our nations must take a number of concerted actions, especially the following:

1. *Reduction of dependence on imported oil and gas*

The United States and Canada should aim at being substantially independent, with less than 5 percent of energy demand filled by imported oil and gas, in 1985 and thereafter. Western Europe should reduce dependence to 40 percent, and Japan to 65 percent, by 1985.

2. *Conservation*

All consuming countries should make major efforts for conservation and efficiency of use, holding the annual growth of energy consumption over the next decade below 2 percent in North America, 3 percent in Europe, and 4 percent in Japan. Their peoples should be prepared for even sharper cuts if necessary and for a real (though presumably temporary) reduction in living standards.

3. *Development of new sources*

The common energy strategy should include setting rough national and Trilateral production goals, covering the period to 1985, for coal, oil, natural gas, nuclear power, and other forms of energy. Consequent decisions on investment for increased production, and for research on development of new sources of energy for the longer run, should be taken without delay. The Trilateral countries should plan together for future cooperation in the development of the extensive energy reserves of North America as an important means of meeting the long-run needs of the entire Trilateral area.

4. *Meeting the financial drain*

The consuming countries should recognize the dangers of the current drain on their monetary reserves for oil payments and should do their best to create conditions for a reduction of oil prices. At the same time they should reduce the impact of the crisis through recycling arrangements, emergency loans to the more hard pressed, and cooperation among themselves and with producing countries on the investment of surplus oil funds, meanwhile taking action by conservation and development of alternative sources of energy to reduce the future size of the problem.

These actions will have far-reaching consequences for the structure of our societies and the lives of our citizens. The Trilateral countries, accordingly, should reach broad agreement on what those changes will be and on equitable standards for bearing the burdens of scarcity and adjustment. Both governments and peoples will have to show steadiness and a determination to preserve democratic institutions.

D. EXTERNAL GOALS

1. *Relations with producing countries*

The approach to the oil-producing countries should be based on the common interests and agreed strategy of consuming countries, but should also be attuned to the basic interests of the producers in security, in rapid economic development, and in a larger role in world affairs, and to the common interest of both consumers and producers in a functioning international economy. It is in this context that negotiation should take place on the supply and price of oil.

2. *Arab-Israeli conflict*

Although an Arab-Israeli settlement will not in itself resolve the energy problem, renewed war or failure to reach a settlement could seriously aggravate that problem. The Trilateral countries, following a generally coordinated approach, should use their influence on behalf of steady progress in negotiations between the parties and achievement without undue delay of a peace settlement based on essential acceptance of the principle of non-acquisition of territory by force and the right of all states to secure existence.

E. THE NEED FOR UNITY

The energy crisis has weakened the developed nations and driven them apart. They must re-create their unity. Only if they work together on energy strategy, and on the related problems of finance and trade, will they be able to repair the damage already done and move through the difficult transitional period to a new era of growth based upon dependable sources of energy. In working together they will create, in effect, a Trilateral energy community. In the experience of this constructive enterprise our nations can begin to move the now floundering international economic system to higher and firmer ground.

OPEC, THE TRILATERAL WORLD,

AND THE DEVELOPING COUNTRIES:

NEW ARRANGEMENTS FOR

COOPERATION, 1976-1980

Richard N. Gardner
*Professor of Law
and International
Organization*
Columbia University
New York

Saburo Okita
*President
Overseas Economic
Cooperation Fund*
Tokyo

B. J. Udink
*Former Minister
for Aid to
the Developing
Countries*
The Netherlands

Table of Contents

OPEC, THE TRILATERAL WORLD, AND THE DEVELOPING COUNTRIES:
New Arrangements for Cooperation, 1976-1980

I. INTRODUCTION

In its report entitled "A Turning Point in North-South Economic Relations" the Trilateral Commission Task Force on Relations with Developing Countries proposed a special effort of cooperation between the Trilateral world and the OPEC countries to meet the emergency needs in 1974-75 of some thirty low-income countries of the "Fourth World" who have been particularly hard hit by skyrocketing costs of oil, food, fertilizer and industrial goods. It also outlined some basic concepts that might provide a framework for cooperation between developed and developing countries in the period beyond the short-term emergency. The task force promised to present a specific program to strengthen the multilateral development system in a second report to be issued in the spring of 1975.

To meet the emergency needs of the "Fourth World" in 1974-75, our first report envisaged an emergency program of $3 billion in extra concessional aid, one-half from the Trilateral world, one-half from the OPEC countries. In the months since our report was issued, the proposed Trilateral-OPEC negotiation to produce this shared effort of collaboration has not occurred. Nevertheless, the United Nations has made some progress with its emergency program, launched by the General Assembly at the special session of March-April 1974, to help the most severely affected developing countries. OPEC and Trilateral countries have separately promised substantial increases in their bilateral financial aid programs in response to the UN's appeal, and the United States has announced a significant increase in its food aid. Moreover, medium-term loans from the new "oil facility" of the International Monetary Fund are being made available to some of the most severely affected countries to tide them over their immediate difficulties. One way or another, it appears that the "Fourth World" will manage to get through the 1974-75 period without an economic disaster.

Attention must now be directed to the problem of North-South cooperation in development beyond the emergency period. This problem is much more formidable than that of devising short-term solutions. In his address to the annual meeting of the Board of Governors of the World Bank group on September 30, 1974, Robert S. McNamara estimated that unless ways are found to increase the present level of Official Development Assistance (ODA)[1] in terms of real purchasing power rather than just in money terms the billion people in countries with average incomes under $200 per capita are likely to face a decline in their standard of living amounting to 0.4% per capita per year between now and 1980. To make possible a 2.1% annual growth in their per capita GNP — a modest rate of growth by any standard — would require an increase in ODA, in terms of 1973 dollars, from $9.4 billion in 1973 to $13.5 billion in 1980, an increase of about $4 billion. Taking account of anticipated inflation and the further deterioration in the world economy since McNamara's address which has aggravated even more the problems of the low-income countries, an increase in ODA by $6 billion a year for the years 1976-80 at then-existing prices is the very minimum that seems to be required. (McNamara's detailed estimates on ODA requirements are set out in Annex 1.)

The case for supplying that additional $6 billion per year of ODA for the one billion people in the low-income countries is based on the considerations set forth in the first report of our task force. As we noted there, the Trilateral countries need the developing countries as sources of raw materials, as export markets and, most important of all, as constructive partners in the building of a satisfactory world economic and political order. The world's interrelated crises of population growth, environmental deterioration, mass poverty, mounting unemployment, growing social and political instability, proliferating nuclear and conventional weapons, and escalating terrorism and international conflict cannot be solved without attention to the needs and priorities of the developing as well as the developed world.

There will be increasing pressures to "write off" some of the low-income developing countries in the Indian subcontinent and Africa if the economic and political crises deepen in the Trilateral world. But it is doubtful if the people of the Trilateral countries would find such a

[1]Official Development Assistance is defined as government aid with at least a 25% grant element.

policy to be either morally acceptable or politically realistic if the moment ever came to carry it out. In terms of the long-term interest of the Trilateral world, it would prove ultimately self-destructive.

To these considerations there can now be added another very practical argument. In a time of stagnant growth and rising unemployment, it is clearly in the interest of the Trilateral countries to move funds from OPEC countries which cannot spend them on Trilateral country exports to other developing countries who will. To the extent that aid contributions from the Trilateral world bring forth additional aid contributions from the OPEC countries, they have a multiplier effect on exports, employment and income, also helping the balance of payments. Indeed, we need to think in terms of a second type of "Trilateralism" — by which OPEC countries transfer a portion of their liquid balances in the Trilateral world into long-term loans to the LDCs, who in turn spend the proceeds on Trilateral country exports.

Assuming this case for increasing ODA is sound, two central questions remain to be addressed: First, where is the extra $6 billion a year to come from? Second, what changes in the structure of multilateral development institutions seem to be required?

II. THE FINANCING PROBLEM

A solution to the question of long-term financing is clearly going to require a major act of cooperation between the Trilateral countries and the OPEC countries. To be sure, the OPEC countries have already taken a number of initiatives to increase the flow of concessional aid. Kuwait and Venezuela have substantially increased their existing aid programs. Iran and Iraq are selling a certain amount of oil to India on concessional terms. Saudi Arabia has set up its own Development Fund and has made large commitments of aid to Egypt and other Arab countries. Libya, Abu Dhabi, and the Emirates are increasing their bilateral efforts. In addition, some major multilateral ventures among OPEC nations have been announced — a $200 million Special Arab Fund for Africa, an Arab Bank for Industrial and Agricultural Development in Africa with an initial capital of $200 million, an Islamic Bank with an authorized capital of $2 billion, and an OPEC Fund. The capital of the already-operating Arab Fund for Economic and Social Development is expected to be increased substantially. Taken all together, commitments of concessional aid by OPEC countries in 1974 reached $7.6 billion, although it should be noted that two-thirds of this sum was concentrated on three Arab countries — Egypt, Syria, and Jordan. While it is difficult to make precise estimates of what all this is likely to mean in actual aid disbursements, conversations with knowledgeable officials suggest that total OPEC disbursements of ODA are likely to reach some $3 billion a year in the 1976-80 period. This will still leave a shortfall of $3 billion from the $6 billion of additional ODA each year that is estimated to be required to achieve minimum development goals.

It is highly unlikely that this additional $3 billion a year can be raised between Trilateral and OPEC countries by any of the traditional aid-giving methods. ODA is already in deep trouble in the Trilateral world. During the ten-year period 1963-73, while the real income of citizens of the countries who are members of the OECD's Development Assistance Committee was growing by 60%, the real value of ODA supplied by these countries was actually declining by 7%. During the past year, a number of Trilateral countries have further reduced their ODA in real terms. If the Trilateral countries are to have any credibility in aid discussions with the OPEC countries and the rest of the developing world, they should agree at a minimum to maintain the real value of their ODA for the remainder of this decade, applying an automatic upward adjustment of bilateral and multilateral financial flows to keep pace with inflation. Just to do this will require a formidable effort of political leadership. It is hard to envisage the Trilateral countries increasing their existing programs to cover any substantial portion of the $3 billion a year ODA shortfall that will still remain.

The prospect of securing the $3 billion shortfall in ODA from the OPEC countries is not much better. This shortfall is already estimated on the basis of a $3 billion annual ODA effort of the OPEC countries through their own bilateral and regional programs. A $3 billion annual aid program would represent close to 2% of the combined GNP of the OPEC countries (a good deal more for individual OPEC donors like Iran and the Persian Gulf states) compared to average existing aid levels of .30% of GNP for Trilateral countries. To put it differently, the combined GNP of the OPEC countries (exclusive of Nigeria and Indonesia, whose income of around $100 per capita even with increased oil revenues will exempt them from any substantial aid-giving) is forecast by the World Bank at only 6% of the combined GNP of the Trilateral countries as late as 1980. If the OPEC countries give $3 billion a year of ODA in the years 1976-80 and the Trilateral countries maintain the real value of their existing aid levels, the ODA of OPEC countries will be about 20% of Trilateral levels during this period. If they are challenged to increase their ODA substantially to take up all or even half of the $3 billion shortfall, they are likely to reply that they are already doing much more than their share in terms of conventional burden-sharing formulae. Indeed, they will probably make the further argument that additional ODA burdens for them are particularly inappropriate, since they involve financial transfers from a resource base of oil that is being depleted, whereas the Trilateral countries can finance ODA from an industrial base whose output renews itself and even grows with each passing year.

The conclusion seems inescapable that an agreed sharing of the $3 billion in extra ODA per year is unlikely to be found except through a wholly new approach. Such an approach would start with the recognition that the relevant characteristics of the OPEC countries differ so fundamentally from those of the traditional aid donors that an attempt to share ODA on the basis of percentages of GNP will neither produce a sense of rough justice as between the Trilateral and OPEC groups or the necessary volume of financial flows. The Trilateral countries represent an annual GNP of nearly $3 trillion, but as a group cannot generate large amounts of foreign exchange. The OPEC countries represent $150-200 billion of GNP but are running current account surpluses of over $50 billion a year (although some estimates suggest these surpluses will decline substantially and even disappear by the end of the decade). A new approach would proceed on the basis that the OPEC countries, being highly liquid but not yet rich, should provide a disproportionately large amount of the extra financial flows with a disproportionately small concessional aid element, while the Trilateral countries, being still very rich but not very liquid, should supply a disproportionately small amount of the extra financial flows with a disproportionately large concessional aid element.

One of the most politically attractive ways of combining OPEC and Trilateral resources along these lines would be through an interest subsidy, subscribed by the Trilateral and OPEC countries, to transform large amounts of lending from OPEC countries on commercial terms into ODA on terms suitable to low-income countries. To be specific: a new "Third Window" could be opened in the World Bank alongside its regular lending operations and those of the International Development Association. The managers of the "Third Window" would borrow the $3 billion estimated to be required each year at an interest rate of 8% and lend the money to low-income countries at 3% (very easy terms at present rates of inflation). The $3 billion would be raised by issuing bonds directly to OPEC governments or in the capital markets of Trilateral countries where substantial OPEC funds are available.

According to studies by the World Bank staff, it requires a subsidy fund of 23.45% of the face value of a loan to subsidize a 5% interest differential for project lending (slow disbursement) and a subsidy fund of 34.61% of the face value of a loan for program lending (more rapid disbursement), assuming loans to low-income countries with 20-year maturities and 4-year grace periods. The required subsidy fund increases, of course, if easier repayment schedules are permitted. But lending on the basis described above could meet the needs of many of the low-income countries in view of the fact that the present rate of inflation reduces the burden of repayment and of the fact that the IDA would continue its own more concessional lending program of 50-year loans with 10-year grace periods and only a ¾ of 1% service charge. It should also be noted that very poor countries like Bangladesh could get additional IDA money if the relatively better-off IDA recipients were given access to "Third Window" loans instead. "Third Window" money could finance both general development programs and specific projects, with special emphasis on projects in agriculture and energy, where there is now a very considerable scope for productive investment. Given a blend of project and program lending, the subsidy needed would be about 30% of the annual lending or about $900 million a year. (For calculations of the subsidy required under different assumptions of interest-rate differentials, maturities and grace periods, see Annex 2.)

Some $100 million of this amount could be provided each year from the profits of the World Bank's regular loan operations. Of the remaining $800 million a year, $500 million might be provided by the Trilateral countries, and $300 million by the OPEC countries. The precise division of the burden would, of course, be a matter for negotiation.

The most obvious political advantage of this proposal is that comparatively small amounts of additional resources would be required from any one country. For example, based on the burden-sharing formula used in the fourth IDA replenishment, the yearly share of the subsidy fund for the nine members of the European Community would be about $190 million; for Japan, about $55 million; for the United States, about $170 million; for Canada, about $30 million; with other IDA contributors making up the rest (about $55 million). An American President could point out to Congress that the relatively small sum of $170 million, supplemented by contributions from other Trilateral countries, was moving $3 billion of extra OPEC funds to the low-income countries.

Further in support of the proposal it could be argued that moving $3 billion from OPEC countries unable to spend it to low-income countries who were able to do so would stimulate employment and income in the Trilateral world. Based on the fact that from one-quarter to one-third of procurement from World Bank group lending has been in the U.S., the $170 million U.S. contribution could mean $750 million to $1 billion in additional U.S. exports. Other Trilateral countries could enjoy a similar "multiplier-effect" on their exports from their contributions to the interest subsidy.

In return for these advantages, of course, it should be clearly understood that under the "Third Window" plan the Trilateral countries, who account at present for about 75% of the World Bank's capital subscriptions, would be carrying the main burden as guarantors for the repayment of moneys borrowed from OPEC countries and re-lent to low-income developing countries. Why, it may be asked, should the Trilateral countries assume such an obligation? Should not OPEC countries be asked to assume the risk of lending themselves? The answer to this question is, first, that the OPEC countries are not likely to assume such a risk for an additional $3 billion of lending beyond their estimated $3 billion in concessional aid and, second, that the "Third Window" proposal involves a "package deal" that serves the interests of all the countries involved.

The industrialized countries, the non-oil-producing developing countries, and the OPEC countries have a shared interest in the latter's participation in multilateral development institutions. The first two groups benefit because the multilateral institutions secure the increased resources they need to function effectively and to avoid being gradually eclipsed by OPEC-country institutions with aid programs that are not only geographically limited but often politically linked. The OPEC countries benefit by being able to invest in the obligations of multilateral institutions backed by the guarantees of the rest of the world's economic powers; they also get a "buffer" between themselves and low-income developing countries who might prove difficult when it comes to repaying loans or using aid effectively. All sides also get a chance to develop a working partnership in the financial field that may eventually lead to more satisfactory negotiations in other areas, including energy questions and oil prices.

Another question that may arise in connection with the "Third Window" proposal is how such a comparatively modest subsidy fund can finance such large amounts of capital flows. The answer is that if the subsidy fund is made available each year in the specified amounts only a small portion will actually be needed to cover the interest payments and the remainder of the subsidy fund can be invested at commercial rates (8% is assumed in the estimates given above). Moreover, and this point should be faced frankly, the estimates assume, in accordance with normal World Bank group lending experience, that there is some lag each year between the new money being made available by the OPEC countries and the actual disbursements from the "Third Window." Thus there is an 8% interest cost only on that portion of the $3 billion annual borrowing that is actually disbursed to the low-income countries. In short, the normal disbursement schedule of multilateral lending agencies means that something less than the full $3 billion a year will be coming to the low-income countries in the first years of the plan.

To take care of this problem, some increased medium-term lending will be needed from the IMF "oil facility" in the early years of the plan. To facilitate IMF lending to the low-income countries at rates well below the 7% IMF rate, another much smaller "subsidy fund" may have to be contemplated. The Fund's Interim Committee has recommended the establishment of a "special account" to reduce the burden of interest payments on "oil facility" loans to the most severely affected developing countries, but it is not clear where the funds for the "special account" will come from. One possibility to be considered is the use of profits from the sale of small amounts of the Fund's gold holdings on the private market. The amounts needed for the "special account" would be a good deal less than the $900 million annual subsidy fund required for the "Third Window" because the loans would be shorter-term and the volume of lending less. The gold sales required for this purpose would not unduly depress the free market gold price. Fears on this score have caused some Fund members to oppose sales of Fund gold in the past. While gold sales would probably be opposed as a means of raising the $900 million interest subsidy for the "Third Window," agreement might be possible on selling the more modest amounts needed to subsidize "oil facility" lending to low-income countries in a transitional period while the "Third Window" was getting underway.

Influenced in part by an earlier version of this paper, the new IMF/IBRD Development Committee, consisting of Finance Ministers from 20 countries, has called for a study of the "Third Window" plan. It is hoped that sufficient support can be obtained in the months ahead from Trilateral, OPEC and other countries so that the "Third Window" with its urgently needed development funds will be ready to begin operations at the outset of the 1976-80 period.

III. THE RESTRUCTURING PROBLEM

The problem of institutional restructuring is directly related to the financing problem. The OPEC countries are unlikely to participate in the kind of multilateral venture described above unless they come in as full partners with the Trilateral countries, with voting and other arrangements reflecting the financial contributions they are being asked to make. In the Fund and Bank as they are presently organized, the OPEC countries have quotas and voting rights equal to 5% of the total. The Arab members of OPEC have quotas and voting rights equal to 2% of the total — roughly the share of Belgium. The OPEC countries are not likely to regard these arrangements as a satisfactory basis for their expanded participation in multilateral financial arrangements under Fund or Bank auspices. (The existing distribution of quotas and voting rights in the Fund and of subscriptions and voting rights in the Bank are shown in Annex 3.)

One approach to this structural problem would be to increase the quotas and voting rights of the OPEC countries in the Fund and Bank to reflect their new economic power. In the quinquennial review of Fund quotas that is now underway, a decision has been reached to increase the total OPEC percentage to about 10% of the total. This would still be less than half of the voting power presently enjoyed by the United States alone or by the countries of the European Community as a group.

A larger increase in the OPEC share seems to face opposition for several reasons. First, the traditional indicators relied on in these quota reviews (GNP and trade statistics with foreign exchange reserves only one of several factors) do not justify a larger increase. Second, and clearly more important, there is resistance on the part of most Fund members (developing as well as developed) to accept reductions in their percentages to make possible more than modest OPEC increases. The United States, in particular, which now has 21% of the votes in the Fund, is reluctant to lose its present veto power on amendments to the Fund Articles, which require the approval of three-fifths of the members with 80% of the voting power. Third, there appears to be some fear that a more substantial increase in the OPEC share — to 15% or more, for example — would give the OPEC countries a veto over the issuance or cancellation of SDRs (which require an 85% vote) and even over amendments, given the financial leverage of OPEC countries over other Fund members.

The general interest of the membership of the Fund and Bank, including that of the Trilateral countries, would seem to indicate a more forthcoming attitude toward increases in the quotas and voting rights of OPEC countries. Traditional indicators used in previous quota reviews are not sufficient guides in the radically new situation in which the world now finds itself, where the OPEC countries may soon dispose of half the world's monetary reserves and where they are being asked to make major financial contributions to IMF recycling plans and to the purchase of World Bank bonds. In the light of these considerations, an increase in the OPEC share to between 15 and 20% in the Fund and Bank would seem more appropriate than the 10% now envisaged. The larger quota increases would mean more OPEC funds available for the Fund and Bank's regular operations. The increased voting power of OPEC would pose no real threat of an "OPEC veto" since the OPEC countries have not voted as a block on financial and development matters (except, of course, to the extent that they vote in solidarity as members of the group of developing countries, which already have sufficient votes to block SDR allocations or amendments).

In the World Bank, it should be noted, the voting majority required for the approval of loans is 50% (actual votes are very rare). As major contributors, OPEC countries are likely to be prudent in their judgment of loan proposals. In any event, a 15-20% OPEC voting share would not fundamentally alter the balance of power in the Bank's Executive Board; the Trilateral countries would still have over half the votes on a weighted-voting basis.

In reaching its decision to increase the OPEC share to 10% in Fund quotas and voting rights, the Fund's Interim Committee has wisely agreed that the next review of quotas and voting rights should take place within three rather than the usual five years. For the reasons suggested above, it would be useful if the Trilateral countries could indicate now their sympathetic interest in seeing the OPEC countries' share raised to 15-20% at that time, assuming, of course, that the OPEC countries are willing to assume increased responsibilities in the Fund, e.g., by continuing their contributions to recycling efforts through the Fund's "oil facility" and permitting their currencies to be used for regular Fund lending (several OPEC members do not yet do so).

The World Bank has traditionally adjusted shares of subscriptions and voting rights in accordance with decisions reached in the quota reviews of the Fund. In the special circumstances of the present time, however, there are good reasons for increasing the OPEC countries' share in the Bank beyond the 10% agreed to in the Fund to the 15-20%

figure suggested earlier, without waiting for the next review of Fund quotas in three years. Given the differences in the character of the two institutions, there is no reason why the distribution of contributions and voting rights must be identical. As a practical matter, it would be advantageous to have a larger OPEC country share in World Bank subscriptions as soon as possible. This would add to the Bank's paid-in capital and increase the share of OPEC countries in the guaranteeing of Bank obligations.

Yet even an immediate 15-20% share for OPEC countries in the Bank's regular operations would not solve the problem of providing them with an adequate voice in the management of the $3 billion-a-year "Third Window" program for the low-income countries that has been proposed above. Under the Bank's Articles of Agreement, all Bank loans must remain the responsibility of the Bank's Executive Board, where the regular distribution of voting shares applies. But there is no reason why special arrangements could not be devised for the management of the subsidy fund, where the managers of the fund could make decisions on the types of loans to be subsidized or even on subsidies to particular loans on a case-by-case basis. In effect, there would be a bicameral arrangement, with the Bank's Executive Board approving loan proposals and the "Third Window" management deciding on the disposition of the subsidy fund.

These special arangements for the "Third Window" could be modeled after those suggested by the Shah of Iran at the beginning of 1974. The Shah proposed a special fund associated with the World Bank which would have a governing body composed equally of representatives from developed countries, from OPEC countries, and from other developing countries. This tripartite approach would seem to be a reasonable one, considering the large OPEC contribution to the special concessional aid operation here proposed (all of the $3 billion each year plus $300 million of the $900 million annual subsidy), and considering also the legitimate interest of other developing countries in the management of the "Third Window" program. The day-to-day administration of the subsidy fund and of lending operations facilitated by it would be carried out by the officers and staff of the World Bank group, which represents a concentration of experience and technical skill that would not be easy to duplicate.

More than changes in voting arrangements and formal managerial structures may be required, however, to provide the OPEC countries, and particularly the Arab members of OPEC, with confidence in the World Bank group and its new "Third Window." To begin with, there should be greater attention to Arab sensibilities in the scheduling of meetings (the 1974 Annual Meetings of the Bank and Fund were scheduled on Ramadan). Special courses, some of them in Arabic, should be organized by the Bank's Economic Development Institute in a major effort to train bright young leaders from OPEC countries for service with the World Bank group or for comparable responsibilities in their own governments. Gradually, the top management of the Bank and Fund ought to include a larger number of OPEC country nationals, including nationals from Arab countries.

Such a restructuring of the world's major international financial institutions will not be easy — no major adjustment of established organizations ever is. But it will provide a major test of the willingness of the Trilateral world to come to terms with new economic realities and to share power with those whose cooperation is now essential to preserve a working world economy. For the reasons suggested earlier, the Trilateral world, the OPEC countries, and the developing countries seeking development aid all have an interest in a successful solution to the restructuring problem.

IV. OTHER QUESTIONS

Even with a major new effort of multilateral cooperation along the lines proposed above, the bulk of industrialized and OPEC country aid efforts will continue to be through bilateral and regional channels. It would be useful to have a forum in which the industrialized and OPEC countries could exchange information and discuss aid policy questions, including aid levels and terms, types of projects to be supported, and distribution among recipient countries. Possible forums to be considered for this purpose are the new IMF/IBRD Development Committee, which includes recipient developing countries; the Development Assistance Committee (DAC) of the OECD, which includes only industrialized countries, but which could be broadened to include OPEC donors; or some new forum to be specially created. Pending the decision on a forum, OPEC countries could be invited to participate on an *ad hoc* basis in DAC meetings and in OECD and World Bank consortia and consultative groups. Moreover, if the mandate of OPEC could be broadened to include aid questions, useful cooperation could be developed between the OECD and World Bank staffs, on the one hand, and the OPEC secretariat on the other.

172

There is a real danger that in concentrating on the approximately 30 low-income countries of the "Fourth World" there will be a tendency to neglect the very real problems of the new "middle class" — countries like Mexico, Brazil, Turkey, Malaysia and the Republic of Korea. These nations have made rapid progress in the past, but they are likely to face serious financial problems in the future due to the higher cost of food and fuel, particularly if slow growth in the Trilateral world dims prospects for their exports. Substantial amounts of financing between commercial lending and ODA may be needed if the recent gains of these countries are not to be jeopardized. This could take the form of conventional World Bank lending and also loans from the IMF "oil facility," which may need to be continued beyond 1975 for this purpose as well as for aid to Trilateral countries.

Before concluding, special emphasis should be placed on the desirability of including the Soviet Union in multilateral development efforts, not only in the interest of detente and global solidarity, but because the Soviet Union has substantial economic capabilities and has benefited from the increase in raw material prices. Full Soviet membership in the Fund and Bank system seems unlikely in the near future, but the U.S.S.R. should certainly be invited to participate in the interest subsidy for the $3 billion fund in the World Bank's "Third Window," or in some parallel UN effort whose activities could be coordinated with those of the World Bank group. During the cold war era, the Soviet Union remained outside of multilateral development efforts. In a new era concerned with global survival, every effort should be made to include it.

ANNEX 1
Flow of Official Development Assistance Measured as a Percent of Gross National Product[a]

Country	1960	1965	1970	1971	1972	1973	1974	1975	1980[d] Required Case I	Case II
Australia	.38	.53	.59	.53	.59	.44	.53	.54		
Austria		.11	.07	.07	.08	.13	.13	.13		
Belgium	.88	.60	.46	.50	.55	.51	.56	.62		
Canada	.19	.19	.42	.42	.47	.43	.51	.51		
Denmark	.09	.13	.38	.43	.45	.47	.49	.50		
France	1.38	.76	.66	.66	.67	.58	.55	.51		
Germany	.31	.40	.32	.34	.31	.32	.30	.28		
Italy	.22	.10	.16	.18	.09	.14	.10	.08		
Japan	.24	.27	.23	.23	.21	.25	.24	.24		
Netherlands[b]	.31	.36	.61	.58	.67	.54	.61	.65		
New Zealand					.23	.27	.36	.47		
Norway	.11	.16	.32	.33	.41	.45	.47	.42		
Portugal	1.45	.59	.67	1.42	1.79	.71	.63	.65		
Sweden	.05	.19	.38	.44	.48	.56	.69	.70		
Switzerland	.04	.09	.15	.11	.21	.15	.15	.15		
United Kingdom	.56	.47	.37	.41	.39	.35	.34	.32		
United States[c]	.53	.49	.31	.32	.29	.23	.21	.20		
GRAND TOTALS										
ODA $ millions (current prices)	4665	5895	6832	7762	8671	9415	10706	11948	16760	24400
ODA 1973 prices	7660	9069	9346	9976	10059	9415	9391	9452	9259	13480
GNP $ billions (current prices)	898	1340	2010	2218	2550	3100	3530	4100	8200	8200
ODA as % GNP	.52	.44	.34	.35	.34	.30	.30	.29	.20	.30
ODA Deflator	60.9	65.0	73.1	77.8	86.2	100.0	114.0	126.4	181.0	181.0

[a]Countries included are members of OECD Development Assistance Committee, accounting for more than 95% of total Official Development Assistance. Figures for 1973 and earlier years are actual data. The projections for 1974 and 1975 are based on World Bank estimates of growth of GNP, on information on budget appropriations for aid, and on aid policy statements made by governments. Because of the relatively long period of time required to translate legislative authorizations first into commitments and later into disbursements, it is possible to project today, with reasonable accuracy, ODA flows (which by definition represent disbursements) through 1975.

[b]New Zealand became a member of the DAC only in 1973. ODA figures for New Zealand are not available for 1960-71.

[c]In 1949, at the beginning of the Marshall Plan, U.S. Official Development Assistance amounted to 2.79% of GNP.

[d]Case I leading to a — 0.4% change in GNP per capita per annum in countries with incomes of under $200 per capita would require ODA of $16.7 billion (.20% of DAC GNP) in 1980; Case II with 2.1% growth in GNP per capita would require $24.4 billion (.30% of DAC GNP) in that year.

Source: Robert S. McNamara, Address to the Board of Governors of the World Bank Group, September 30, 1974.

ANNEX 2
Subsidy Fund Required (% of face value of loan)

Loan Type	Maturity (years)	Grace (years)	Interest Differential Paid by Subsidy Fund		
			3%	4%	5%
Project	20	4	14.07%	18.76%	23.45%
Program (more rapid disbursement)	20	4	20.77%	27.69%	34.61%
Project (extended grace period)	20	7	15.33%	20.44%	25.55%
Project (extended maturity)	35	4	21.40%	28.54%	35.67%
Project (extended grace and maturity)	35	10	22.36%	29.81%	37.26%

Source: World Bank staff calculations

175

Existing Distribution of Voting Power in the IMF and IBRD

Member	International Monetary Fund		International Bank for Reconstruction and Development	
	Quota (% of total)	Voting Power (% of total)	Subscription (% of total)	Voting Power (% of total)
Afghanistan	.13	.19	.12	.19
Algeria	.45	.48	.43	.47
Argentina	1.51	1.44	1.46	1.39
Australia	2.28	2.13	2.22	2.06
Austria	.92	.91	.90	.89
Bahamas	.07	.14	.07	.15
Bahrain	.03	.11	.03	.12
Bangladesh	.43	.46	.42	.46
Barbados	.04	.12	.04	.13
Belgium	2.23	2.09	2.17	2.02
Bolivia	.13	.19	.08	.16
Botswana	.02	.09	.02	.10
Brazil	1.51	1.44	1.46	1.39
Burma	.21	.26	.20	.26
Burundi	.07	.14	.06	.14
Cameroon	.12	.19	.08	.16
Canada	3.77	3.48	3.69	3.37
Central African Republic	.04	.12	.04	.12
Chad	.04	.12	.04	.12
Chile	.54	.57	.37	.42
China	1.88	1.78	2.94	2.70
Colombia	.54	.56	.37	.41
Congo, People's Republic of	.04	.12	.04	.12
Costa Rica	.11	.18	.04	.12
Cyprus	.09	.16	.09	.16
Dahomey	.04	.12	.04	.12
Denmark	.89	.88	.87	.86
Dominican Republic	.15	.21	.06	.14
Ecuador	.11	.18	.07	.15
Egypt, Arab Republic of	.64	.66	.56	.58
El Salvador	.12	.19	.05	.13
Equatorial Guinea	.03	.10	.03	.11
Ethiopia	.09	.16	.04	.13
Fiji	.04	.12	.04	.13
Finland	.65	.66	.63	.65
France	5.14	4.72	5.01	4.55
Gabon	.05	.12	.05	.13
Gambia, The	.02	.10	.02	.11
Germany, Federal Republic of	5.48	5.02	5.34	4.85
Ghana	.30	.35	.29	.34
Greece	.47	.50	.29	.34
Guatemala	.12	.19	.05	.13
Guinea	.08	.15	.08	.16
Guyana	.07	.14	.07	.15
Haiti	.07	.14	.06	.14
Honduras	.09	.15	.03	.12
Iceland	.08	.15	.07	.15
India	3.22	2.98	3.52	3.23
Indonesia	.89	.88	.86	.85
Iran	.66	.67	.62	.64
Iraq	.37	.41	.27	.33
Ireland	.41	.45	.40	.45
Israel	.45	.48	.43	.47
Italy	3.43	3.17	3.34	3.06
Ivory Coast	.18	.24	.14	.21
Jamaica	.18	.24	.17	.24
Japan	4.11	3.79	4.00	3.65
Jordan	.08	.15	.07	.15
Kenya	.16	.23	.16	.23
Khmer Republic	.09	.15	.08	.16

Member	International Monetary Fund		International Bank for Reconstruction and Development	
	Quota (% of total)	Voting Power (% of total)	Subscription (% of total)	Voting Power (% of total)
Korea	.27	.32	.27	.33
Kuwait	.22	.28	.27	.33
Laos	.04	.12	.04	.12
Lebanon	.03	.11	.04	.12
Lesotho	.02	.09	.02	.10
Liberia	.10	.17	.08	.16
Libyan Arab Republic	.08	.15	.08	.16
Luxembourg	.07	.14	.08	.16
Malagasy Republic	.09	.16	.09	.16
Malawi	.05	.12	.06	.14
Malaysia	.64	.65	.62	.64
Mali	.08	.15	.07	.15
Malta	.05	.13	—	—
Mauritania	.04	.12	.04	.12
Mauritius	.08	.15	.07	.15
Mexico	1.27	1.22	.89	.88
Morocco	.39	.43	.38	.42
Nepal	.04	.12	.04	.13
Netherlands	2.40	2.24	2.32	2.15
New Zealand	.69	.70	.67	.69
Nicaragua	.09	.16	.04	.12
Niger	.04	.12	.04	.12
Nigeria	.46	.49	.45	.49
Norway	.82	.82	.80	.80
Oman	.02	.10	.02	.11
Pakistan	.81	.80	.78	.78
Panama	.12	.19	.07	.15
Paraguay	.07	.14	.02	.11
Peru	.42	.46	.29	.34
Philippines	.53	.56	.52	.55
Portugal	.40	.44	.31	.37
Qatar	.07	.14	.07	.15
Romania	.65	.66	.63	.65
Rwanda	.07	.14	.06	.14
Saudi Arabia	.46	.49	.45	.49
Senegal	.12	.18	.13	.20
Sierra Leone	.09	.15	.06	.14
Singapore	.13	.19	.13	.20
Somalia	.07	.14	.06	.14
South Africa	1.10	1.07	1.07	1.04
Spain	1.35	1.30	1.32	1.26
Sri Lanka	.34	.38	.32	.38
Sudan	.25	.30	.23	.30
Swaziland	.03	.10	.03	.11
Sweden	1.11	1.08	1.09	1.05
Syrian Arab Republic	.17	.23	.16	.23
Tanzania	.14	.21	.14	.21
Thailand	.46	.49	.45	.49
Togo	.05	.12	.06	.14
Trinidad and Tobago	.22	.27	.21	.27
Tunisia	.16	.23	.15	.22
Turkey	.52	.54	.50	.54
Uganda	.14	.20	.13	.20
United Arab Emirates	.05	.12	.05	.13
United Kingdom	9.59	8.74	10.18	9.15
United States	22.95	20.80	25.34	22.66
Upper Volta	.04	.12	.04	.12
Uruguay	.24	.29	.16	.23
Venezuela	1.13	1.10	.77	.77
Viet-Nam	.21	.27	.21	.28
Western Samoa	.01	.08	.01	.09
Yemen Arab Republic	.03	.11	.03	.12
Yemen, People's Democratic Republic of	.10	.17	.10	.17
Yugoslavia	.71	.72	.46	.50
Zaire	.39	.43	.38	.42
Zambia	.26	.31	.21	.27
Totals*	100.00	100.00	100.00	100.00

*May differ from the sum of the individual percentages shown because of rounding.

APPENDICES

The Rapporteurs

Trilateral Monetary Task Force

RICHARD N. COOPER has been appointed Under Secretary of State for Economic Affairs in the new U.S. Administration. He was Professor of Economics at Yale University, where he also served as Provost at the time the trilateral report was written.

MOTOO KAJI is Professor of Economics at Tokyo University, where he has taught since 1955. His latest book is *Gendai no Kokusai Kinyu* (Contemporary International Monetary Affairs).

CLAUDIO SEGRÉ is with the Compagnie Européenne de Placements in Paris. He has worked on the staff of the Commission of the European Communities, and was chairman of its group of experts (1965-67) on the development of a European capital market.

Trilateral Political Task Force

FRANÇOIS DUCHÊNE is Director of the Centre for Contemporary European Studies at the University of Sussex. At the time the trilateral report was written, he was Director of the International Institute of Strategic Studies in London.

KINHIDE MUSHAKOJI is Vice Rector for Programs of the United Nations University in Tokyo. At the time the task force report was prepared, he was Director of the Institute of International Relations for Advanced Studies on Peace and Development in Asia, at Sophia University in Tokyo.

HENRY D. OWEN is coordinating American government preparations for the May 1977 "summit" of industrialized countries. He is on leave as Director of the Foreign Policy Studies Program of the Brookings Institution.

Trilateral Task Force on Relations with Developing Countries

RICHARD N. GARDNER has been appointed U.S. Ambassador to Italy. He was Henry L. Moses Professor of Law and International Organization at Columbia University at the time the task force was at work.

SABURO OKITA has just completed his term as President of Japan's Overseas Economic Cooperation Fund, and is a candidate for election to the House of Councillors. He has been President and Chairman of the Japan Economic Research Center.

B. J. UDINK has served in the Dutch Cabinet as Minister for Aid to Developing Countries (1967-71). He is currently Managing Director of OGEM Holding, N.V. in Rotterdam.

Trilateral Task Force on Trade

GUIDO COLONNA DI PALIANO was a member of the Commission of the European Communities (1964-70). He is now President of La Rinascente, the Italian department store chain.

PHILIP H. TREZISE was U.S. Ambassador to the OECD (1966-69) and Assistant Secretary of State for Economic Affairs (1969-71). He is now a Senior Fellow at the Brookings Institution.

NOBUHIKO USHIBA was Ambassador of Japan to the United States (1970-73), after serving as Vice-Minister of Foreign Affairs. He remains an adviser to the Foreign Minister.

Trilateral Task Force on the Political and International Implications of the Energy Crisis

JOHN C. CAMPBELL has been a Senior Research Fellow at the Council on Foreign Relations since 1955. He had previously served for a number of years in the State Department.

GUY DE CARMOY is Professor at the European Institute of Business Administration (INSEAD) at Fontainebleau. He is the author of *Le Dossier européen de l'energie* (1971) and many other works.

SHINICHI KONDO was Ambassador of Japan to Canada (1969-72) after serving as Deputy Vice-Minister of Foreign Affairs. He is an Adviser to the Board of Directors of the Mitsubishi Corporation.

Summary of the Report of the Monetary Task Force:

Towards a Renovated World Monetary System

Monetary anarchy must not be allowed to undermine the confidence in prosperity built up over two decades, nor to produce a new period of restrictions and mutual hostility from entrenched national positions.

Accordingly, it is the view of the rapporteurs that governments should proceed with dispatch to renovate the international monetary system.

The longer range reforms should include:

i) Improvement of the balance of payments adjustment process, with provision for smaller and prompter changes in exchange rates;

ii) Confirmation of the central role as primary reserves of an international fiduciary issue, renamed *bancor,* to satisfy world liquidity needs and gradually to supplant other forms of reserve assets;

iii) Creation of a new facility, to be lodged in the IMF, for emergency short-term lending to counter speculation and other disruptive capital movements;

iv) Consolidation of foreign exchange reserves, initially on an optional basis, into a new account at the IMF;

v) Establishment of new and effective consultative machinery, within the IMF, to oversee the functioning of the renovated international monetary system and to encourage the coordination and consistency of domestic economic policies.

The rapporteurs also believe that governments should take a number of interim steps to help restore order and stability to the international monetary system. They should:

i) Commit themselves to coordinated intervention in exchange markets if necessary to prevent erratic movements in exchange rates;

ii) Enlarge and multilateralize short-term lending facilities to offset large speculative movements of funds;

iii) Consolidate, on a basis that can later be taken over by the International Monetary Fund, the excessive official holdings of dollars and other foreign exchange;

iv) Indicate their willingness both to support the Eurodollar market and to subject it to close surveillance;

v) Sell gold, on a cooperative and coordinated basis, into private markets, with gains to be transferred to international financial institutions for development assistance.

The Trilateral Process

The report which follows is the joint responsibility of the three rapporteurs of the Trilateral Task Force on Monetary Problems, with Mr. Richard N. Cooper serving as the principal drafter.

Although only the three rapporteurs are responsible for the analysis and recommendations, they were aided in their task by joint or individual consultations held during 1973 in New York City, Washington, Tokyo, Anchorage, Sicily and Paris, which at various stages of the report included a number of government officials as well as the following:

Raymond Barre, *Professor and former Commissioner of the EEC, Paris*
C. Fred Bergsten, *Senior Fellow, the Brookings Institution*
Zbigniew Brzezinski, *Director, the Trilateral Commission*
Sir Alec Cairncross, *Master, St. Peter's College, Oxford University*
Herbert Giersch, *Director, Weltwirtschaftlicher Institut, Kiel University*
David L. Grove, *Vice President and Chief Economist, IBM*
Tadashi Iino, *Counselor, Mitsui Bank; former Executive Vice President, Mitsui Bank*
Yves-André Istel, *Kuhn Loeb & Company*
Yusuke Kashiwagi, *Vice President, Bank of Tokyo*
A. Lamfalussy, *Chairman, Steering Committee, Banque de Bruxelles*
Haruo Maekawa, *Deputy President, Export/Import Bank of Japan*
Saburo Okita, *President, Overseas Economic Cooperation Fund, Tokyo*
Giuseppe Petrilli, *Professor and President of IRI*
Grant Reuber, *Dean, Social Sciences, University of West Ontario*
Takuji Shimano, *Professor of Economics*
M. E. Streit, *Professor, University of Mannheim*
Pierre Uri, *Professor, the Atlantic Institute, Paris*
Takeshi Watanabe, *Japanese Chairman, the Trilateral Commission*

SCHEDULE OF MEETINGS AND CONSULTATIONS:

1. Trilateral rapporteurs' meeting (with Brzezinski), Washington, June 23-24.

2. Consultations between Mr. Cooper and Messrs. Kaji and Watanabe concerning the preliminary drafts, Tokyo, July 23-24.

3. Meeting of Messrs. Cooper, Kaji, Segré, Watanabe, and Brzezinski, Anchorage, August 11-12.

4. Meeting of the North American task force concerning the preliminary draft, August 22.

5. Meeting of the Japanese task force concerning the preliminary draft, September 3.

6. Consultations between Mr. Segré and European monetary experts concerning the preliminary draft, Sicily, September 16.

7. Final trilateral drafting session of the rapporteurs, additional consultants and Brzezinski, Paris, September 29-30.

Summary of the Report of the Political Task Force:
The Crisis of International Cooperation

Growing interdependence and the inadequacy of present forms of co-operation are the principal features of the contemporary international order. Moreover,

1) Rapid economic growth and the emergence of new means of communication have thrust together hitherto isolated parts of the world and intensified the existing pattern of relations among the developed countries, resulting in acute strains both within and among nations;

2) International interaction has developed furthest among the advanced industrialised areas of North America, Western Europe and Japan; unless these regions cooperate, problems involving money, trade, investment, resources, and peace cannot be tackled effectively; if collective action in this crucial area of interdependence were to fail, there would be little reason to expect it to succeed in other areas where links are more tenuous;

3) Trilateral cooperation, however, has now reached a crossroads on a number of fronts: *security* factors resulting from detente have encouraged unilateralism and a degree of manoeuver in U.S. foreign policy that is frequently detrimental to Japanese and West European interests; the *economic* balance of power has shifted against the United States as Western Europe and Japan have consistently expanded trade and growth, while the U.S. finds itself less willing to shoulder past burdens and increasingly subject to rising protectionist pressures at home; *social and political* changes have led to a new self-assertiveness based on the view that all problems can be solved and it is intolerable if they are not, a view conducive to greater competition both within and among countries; *general interdependence* has increased enormously in such areas as multinational business, air travel, and the vulnerability of all advanced economies to inflation and changes in the supply of vital resources; finally, *welfare* considerations have shifted the preoccupation with growth as an end in itself to an awareness of the need for greater governmental direction in shaping growth for social, environmental, and other requirements, thus giving rise to disparities in the policies

and priorities of governments. Faced with these problems, the trilateral regions must either cooperate or allow countries to exploit the 'asymmetries' of the situation for their own national gain;

4) Cooperation between rich and poor remains woefully inadequate, in spite of the network of agencies created after the war to promote development and dramatic increases in aid to the developing world by Japan and Western Europe; there also exists the danger of neo-colonialist *chasses gardées* emanating from regional trade agreements between the advanced countries and the LDC's.

In view of the foregoing analysis:

1) There is a need for new forms of common management and structures of decision-making in order to cope with the requirements of a common future; there is a need, too, for changes in the outlook and habits of humanity for which little has prepared it;

2) The world monetary system must be reformed so as to improve the present system of flexible exchange rates, permit sufficient flexibility to allow for differential economic policies, reinforce recent moves towards a managed international currency, and provide LDC's with more abundant finance;

3) Governments must be held accountable to one another for their actions; at a minimum, they should not be allowed to get away with unilateral or bilateral faits accomplis that are irreversible; more generally, they should take account of their partners' preoccupations when formulating domestic policies; the same applies in relations between the advanced countries and the LDC's;

4) There is an urgent need for an informal public process of collective self-education to generate the joint perspectives from which joint policies can spring;

5) Ultimately, the final aim must be collective action to formalise consultation among the trilateral areas; perhaps an international Advisory Commission headed by, say, three highly respected statesmen can be created in future to clarify political stakes and pave the way for domestic acceptance of concession and compromise;

6) To help achieve these goals, the Trilateral Commission was created with the intention of publishing timely reports on various aspects of contemporary affairs and of involving private citizens in the quest for a more harmonious process of policy development based on trilateral cooperation.

The Trilateral Process

The report which follows is the joint responsibility of the three rapporteurs of the Trilateral Task Force on Political Relations, with Mr. François Duchêne serving as the principal drafter.

Although only the three rapporteurs are responsible for the analysis and conclusions, they were aided in their task by extensive trilateral consultations held during 1973 in Brussels, Tokyo and Washington, which at various stages in the development of the report included a number of government officials as well as the following:

Graham Allison, *Professor of Politics, Harvard University*
Georges Berthoin, *Former Representative of the EEC to the United Kingdom*
Robert R. Bowie, *Professor of International Affairs, Harvard University*
Zbigniew Brzezinski, *Director, The Trilateral Commission*
Peter Dobell, *Director, Parliamentary Center for Foreign Affairs and Foreign Trade, Ottawa*
George S. Franklin, *North American Secretary, The Trilateral Commission*
Wolfgang Hager, *Director of Studies, European Community Institute for University Studies*
Kazushige Hirasawa, *Political Commentator and former Editor, The Japan Times*
Norman Jacobs, *Editor-in-Chief, Foreign Policy Association*
Karl Kaiser, *Director, German Institute for International Affairs*
Antonie Knoppers, *President, Merck & Company*
Max Kohnstamm, *President, European Community Institute for University Studies*
Anthony Lake, *Executive Director, International Voluntary Services*
Cesare Merlini, *Director, Italian Institute of International Affairs*
Kiichi Miyazawa, *LDP Deputy and former Minister of International Trade and Industry*
Yonosuke Nagai, *Professor, Tokyo Institute of Technology*
John Pinder, *Director, Political and Economic Planning Institute, London*
J. Robert Schaetzel, *Former U. S. Ambassador to the EEC*
Isaac Shapiro, *President, Japan Society*
Gerard C. Smith, *North American Chairman, The Trilateral Commission*
Yasuo Takeyama, *Chief Editorial Writer, Nihon Keizai Shimbun*
Pierre Uri, *Professor, Atlantic Institute, Paris*
Jiro Ushio, *President, Ushio Electric, Inc., and Executive Member, Japan Committee for Economic Development (Keizai Doyukai)*
James Woolsey, *Staff Member, Senate Armed Services Committee*
Takeshi Watanabe, *Japanese Chairman, The Trilateral Commission*
Tadashi Yamamoto, *Japanese Secretary, The Trilateral Commission*

SCHEDULE OF MEETINGS AND CONSULTATIONS:

1. Trilateral planning consultations among the three rapporteurs and Brzezinski, by conference call, May 9.

2. Meeting of the North American Task Force and Brzezinski with the European rapporteur and principal drafter, François Duchêne, to discuss the preliminary draft, Washington, June 28.

3. Meetings of the Japanese Task Force with the Japanese rapporteur, Kinhide Mushakoji, June 8 and September 12.

4. Meeting of the European rapporteur and Task Force with Brzezinski to discuss the preliminary draft, Brussels, July 18.

5. Trilateral meeting of the Political Task Force and final trilateral drafting consultations among the rapporteurs, Washington, September 20-21.

A Turning Point in
North-South Economic Relations

The time has come for new policies and new actions by the governments of the Trilateral region in their relations with developing countries. There is a crisis in North-South relations that requires two kinds of responses from the Trilateral governments:

First, there is need for a general restructuring of North-South economic relations for the purpose of creating a more just and workable world economic order. Such a new economic order should include, among other things, greater attention by both developed and developing countries to their growing interdependence, greater respect for the equal rights of all members of the world community under international law, the abolition of "spheres of influence," greater recognition of the differing needs and capabilities of different developing countries, the pursuit of cooperation rather than confrontation, the focusing of development efforts on the poorest segment of populations in developing countries, new rules and arrangements governing access to supplies as well as access to markets, and a restructuring of international economic institutions in the light of new political and economic realities. We propose to deal with the extremely complex questions involved in this restructuring in a later report to be issued early in 1975.

Second, there is need to deal with the desperate plight of nearly one billion people in some 30 resource-poor developing countries whose governments cannot pay the increased bills for oil, food, fertilizer and other products. At least $3 billion in extra concessional aid must be found for these countries in 1974-75 to avoid economic disaster. This situation calls for an extraordinary act of cooperation between the countries of the Trilateral region and the oil exporting countries of OPEC. The former bear a special responsibility because they have a vastly greater total national income and the latter bear a special responsibility because of the dramatic increase in their export earnings and therefore in their capacity to invest sums abroad. We believe it would be reasonable for the Trilateral world as a whole to provide about $1.5 billion of this total, with the OPEC countries providing the other $1.5 billion. In response to the appeal of the Secretary-General of the United Nations, contributions to this special emergency effort could be made through bilateral or multilateral channels and could take the form of cash, concessional sales of food, fertilizer and oil, and the cancellation or postponement of debt repayment. The Soviet Union should be invited to participate in this emergency assistance effort in the light of its considerable economic capabilities and the fact that it has benefited on the whole from the recent increase in raw material prices.

The Trilateral Process

The report which follows is the joint responsibility of the three rapporteurs of the Trilateral Task Force on Relations with Developing Countries, with Professor Richard N. Gardner serving as principal drafter.

Although only the three rapporteurs are responsible for the analysis and conclusions, they were aided in their task by extensive consultations with experts from the trilateral regions, the developing countries, and various international organizations. In each case, the consultants spoke for themselves as individuals and not as the representatives of any institutions to which they belong. Those consulted included the following:

David Aaron, *Foreign Policy Advisor to Senator Walter F. Mondale*
Yasushi Akashi, *Senior Officer, Inter-Agency Affairs, United Nations*
Abdoul Barry, *Regional Director for West Africa, Canadian University Service Overseas, Ouagadougou, Upper Volta*
Robert R. Bowie, *Clarence Dillon Professor of International Affairs, Harvard University*
Zbigniew Brzezinski, *Director, The Trilateral Commission*
William D. Clark, *Director, External Relations, International Bank for Reconstruction and Development*
Gerald L. Curtis, *Director, East Asian Institute, Columbia University*
William D. Dale, *Deputy Managing Director, International Monetary Fund*
Pathe Diagne, *African Studies Center, DePauw University, and the Institut Fondamentale de l'Afrique Noire, Dakar, Senegal*
El-Sayed Dohaia, *International Economic Relations Centre, Institute for National Planning, Cairo, Egypt*
George S. Franklin, *North American Secretary, The Trilateral Commission*

Gordon Goundrey, *Professor of Economics, Memorial University, Newfoundland*

Ravi Gulhati, *Director, Development Economics Department, International Bank for Reconstruction and Development*

Mahbub-ul Haq, *Director, Policy Planning and Program Review Department, International Bank for Reconstruction and Development*

Michael Hoffmann, *Director, International Relations Department, International Bank for Reconstruction and Development*

Richard Holbrooke, *Managing Editor,* Foreign Policy *Magazine*

Lady Barbara Ward Jackson, *Former Albert Schweitzer Professor of International Economic Development, Columbia University*

Neville Kanakaratne, *Ambassador of Sri Lanka to the United States*

Lane Kirkland, *Secretary-Treasurer, AFL-CIO*

Max Kohnstamm, *European Chairman, The Trilateral Commission*

Robert S. McNamara, *President, International Bank for Reconstruction and Development*

Maria Teresa Moraes, *Brazilian lawyer and journalist*

Goran Ohlin, *Professor of Economics, University of Stockholm*

Raimi Ola Ojikutu, *Nigerian human biologist and anthropologist*

Akira Onishi, *Project Manager, International Development Center of Japan*

Samuel L. Parmar, *Professor of Economics, Allahabad University, Allahabad, India*

Felix Peña, *Instituto para la Integracion de America Latina, Buenos Aires, Argentina*

Gustav Ranis, *Director, Economic Growth Center, Yale University*

Krishna Roy, *Advisor, Centro de Estudios de Poblacion, Lima, Peru*

Phillips Ruopp, *Director, International Affairs, Charles F. Kettering Foundation*

Gerard C. Smith, *North American Chairman, The Trilateral Commission*

Ernest Sturc, *Director, Exchange and Trade Relations, International Monetary Fund*

Wouter Tims, *Director, Economic Analysis and Projection Department, International Bank for Reconstruction and Development*

Jan Tinbergen, *Professor, Netherlands School of Economics, Rotterdam*

Constantine V. Vaitsos, *Advisor to the Board, Acuerdo de Cartegena, Lima, Peru*

Cyrus R. Vance, *Partner, Simpson, Thacher & Bartlett*

Takeshi Watanabe, *Japanese Chairman, The Trilateral Commission*

H. Johannes Witteveen, *Managing Director, International Monetary Fund*

Bernard Wood, *Executive Secretary, Canadian Group, The Trilateral Commission*

Montague Yudelman, *Director, Agriculture and Rural Development Department, International Bank for Reconstruction and Development*

Ricardo Zuniga, *Visiting Assistant Professor of Sociology, Queens College, City University of New York*

193

SCHEDULE OF TASK FORCE ACTIVITIES:

December 17, 1973 — Joint meeting of the Task Force on Relations with Developing Countries and the Task Force on Trade, in Washington, to discuss the implications of the oil crisis. Also participating were the Commission Director, the three Chairmen, the Secretaries, and members of the Brookings Institution.

December 18 — Task Force meets to select principal drafter, agree on topics to be treated in the report, and arrange future meetings; discussion with Robert S. McNamara, President of the World Bank.

Late January, 1974 — Gardner and Udink meet in Amsterdam.

March 18 — Gardner, Udink, and Onishi meet in Washington to consult with local members of the Trilateral Commission and with Robert S. McNamara, H. Johannes Witteveen and other officials of the IBRD and the IMF.

March 19 — Gardner, Udink, and Onishi meet with experts from various developing countries at the Belmont Conference Center in Maryland, at a conference arranged by the Overseas Development Council and the Charles F. Kettering Foundation.

March 22 — Gardner, Udink, and Onishi meet with local Trilateral Commission members in New York City.

April 24 — First draft of the report completed and circulated within the Commission.

April 27 — Gardner and Udink meet with various consultants in New York City.

May 22 — Second draft of the report completed and approved by all Rapporteurs.

May 30 — Second draft discussed at North American Commissioners meeting in New York City.

Early June — Third draft completed.

June 25 — Discussion of the report at the Executive Committee meeting in Brussels.

Summary of the Report of the Task Force on Trade:

Directions for World Trade in the Nineteen-Seventies

A major multilateral trade negotiation, as called for by some 100 countries in last year's Tokyo Declaration, is the one most hopeful prospect on the international economic horizon.

This is a time of troubles, when inflation, energy crises, and unprecedented balance of payments problems afflict nearly all nations. The structure of international economic cooperation has already been weakened. It could be pulled down in an ultimately pointless scramble for national advantage. A new GATT round offers the possibility of restoring a sense of common purpose and of strengthening the system of rule and order in world trade.

The backlog of issues for negotiation runs from industrial tariffs, which are by no means irrelevant in spite of progress in reducing them, through agricultural trade, non-tariff distortions, export restrictions, safeguards against import disruption, and reform of the General Agreement itself, to trade relations with the third world.

A major reduction in industrial tariffs is needed, both to bring down obstacles to world trade and also to moderate the discriminatory effect of the emerging Western European free trade area. Pending United States trade legislation would provide the basis to achieve deep reciprocal cuts in outstanding levels of tariffs.

For agricultural trade, which has been neglected in earlier negotiations, the need is to reach a bargain which gives the efficient producers greater access to commercial markets abroad and gives importing nations adequate assurance as to future supplies of key commodities. This means an agreement on holding and managing stocks of cereals as well as on improved conditions of commercial trade. It will require commitments to make gradual but important changes in domestic farm policies. A successful bargain here would have far-reaching implications for international cooperation.

Non-tariff distortions in most cases must be dealt with by revising and tightening international rules of conduct, rather than by straight trade-offs. Since few third world countries can be expected to accept stronger GATT rules, many non-tariff agreements will have to be made on a conditional most-favored-nation basis.

Restrictions on exports, the latest of the non-tariff distortions, must be put under rule. At a minimum, advance consultation and the principle of sharing short supplies should be written into GATT. Even if agreement on this is possible only among the industrial countries, it will be a significant step forward.

The question of new safeguards against disruptive imports can best be answered by introducing into the GATT a mediation procedure, based on specific guidelines. This would leave open the possibility of emergency protection, but it would put restraints on arbitrary or unfounded national actions.

Successful negotiations on agriculture, non-tariff distortions and safeguards would call for substantial revisions in and additions to the General Agreement on Tariffs and Trade. Given that the industrial countries probably will be the only ones ready to assume new commitments, it would be desirable to incorporate these into a supplementary Code which would be open to every nation but which would be operated by those subscribing to it rather than by all 80 contracting parties.

The trade interests of the developing countries will have to be given special attention. An effort should be made to identify third world products for tariff reductions; the General Preference schemes should be improved and the United States and Canada should join Japan and the Western European countries in them; commodity price stabilization agreement possibilities need to be explored afresh; and food reserves against potential famine in developing countries must be created.

This mix of new and old questions foreshadows a lengthy and complex negotiation. Its outcome, nonetheless, could go to make the inescapable fact of economic interdependence far less worrisome and far more tolerable than it seems in 1974.

The Trilateral Process

The report which follows is the joint responsibility of the three rapporteurs of the Trilateral Task Force on Trade, with Mr. Philip H. Trezise serving as principal drafter.

Although only the three rapporteurs are responsible for the analysis and conclusions, they were aided in their task by extensive consultations held during 1973 and 1974 in North America, Europe and Japan. These included discussions with Trilateral Commission members and experts from outside the Commission, including high-level government officials, at meetings held in Washington, San Francisco, Chicago, Toronto, London, Bonn and Tokyo. Among those consulted were the following:

Doris Anderson, *Editor,* Chatelaine *Magazine*
Shogoro Ariga, *Executive Managing Editor, Mitsui and Company*
Russell Bell, *Research Director, Canadian Labour Congress*
Kurt Birrenbach, *Member of the Bundestag*
Robert W. Bonner, Q.C., *Chairman, MacMillan Bloedel, Ltd.*
Zbigniew Brzezinski, *Director, The Trilateral Commission*
A. W. Clausen, *President, Bank of America*
George C. Creber, *President, George Weston, Ltd.*
Emmett Dedmon, *Vice President and Editorial Director, Field Enterprises, Inc.*
Peter C. Dobell, *Director, Parliamentary Center for Foreign Affairs and Foreign Trade, Ottawa*
George S. Franklin, *North American Secretary, The Trilateral Commission*
Wolfgang Hager, *European Secretary, The Trilateral Commission*
Naoji Harada, *Executive Director, Japan Foreign Trade Council*
Kenzo Henmi, *Professor of Agricultural Economics, Tokyo University*
Alan Hockin, *Executive Vice President, Toronto-Dominion Bank*
J. K. Jamieson, *Chairman, Exxon Corporation*
Edgar F. Kaiser, *Chairman, Kaiser Industries Corporation*
Karl Kaiser, *Director, Research Institute, German Society for Foreign Policy*
Lane Kirkland, *Secretary-Treasurer, AFL-CIO*
Max Kohnstamm, *European Chairman, The Trilateral Commission*
H. Krüper, *German Chemical-Paper-Ceramics Workers Union (representing Karl Hauenschild, President of the Union)*
Tatsuzo Mizukami, *President, Japan Foreign Trade Council*
Kenneth D. Naden, *President, National Council of Farmer Cooperatives*
Arne Nielsen, *President and General Manager, Mobil Oil, Canada*
Yoshihisa Ojimi, *Executive Vice President, Arabian Oil Company, Ltd.; former Vice Minister of International Trade and Industry*
Jean-Luc Pepin, P.C., *President, Interimco, Ltd.; former Minister of Industry, Trade and Commerce*

John H. Perkins, *President, Continental Illinois National Bank & Trust Company*

John Pinder, *Director, Political & Economic Planning Institute, London*

Charles W. Robinson, *President, Marcona Corporation*

William M. Roth, *Roth Properties*

Albert Schunk, *German Metal Workers Union (representing Eugen Loderer, President of the Union)*

Gerard C. Smith, *North American Chairman, The Trilateral Commission*

Hans-Günther Sohl, *President, Federal Union of German Industry*

Alexandre Stackhovitch, *Chief Advisor, Foreign Economic Policy, Commission of the European Community*

Fukutaro Watanabe, *Professor of Economics, Gakushuin University*

Takeshi Watanabe, *Japanese Chairman, The Trilateral Commission*

Tadashi Yamamoto, *Japanese Secretary, The Trilateral Commission*

SCHEDULE OF TASK FORCE ACTIVITIES:

December 17, 1973 — Joint meeting of the Task Force on Trade and the Task Force on Relations with Developing Countries, in Washington, to discuss the implications of the oil crisis. Also participating were the Commission Director, the three Chairmen, the Secretaries, and members of The Brookings Institution.

December 18 — Task Force meets to select principal drafter, agree on topics to be treated in the report, and arrange future meetings.

February 6, 1974 — Japanese Trade Task Force meeting, Tokyo.

February 19 — Trade issues discussed at San Francisco regional dinner, with Trezise present.

February 22 — Trade issues discussed at Chicago regional luncheon, with Trezise present.

February - March — Ushiba consults with Japanese consultants and government officials.

Early March — First draft of the report completed.

March 12 — Meeting of European consultants, Bonn.

March 21 — Meeting of the three Rapporteurs and Hager, London.

April 24 — Trade issues discussed at Canadian regional meeting, Toronto; Trezise present.

Early May — Second draft of the report completed and circulated within the Commission.

June 24 — Discussion of the report at the Executive Committee meeting, Brussels.

SUMMARY OF THE FIRST REPORT OF THE TRILATERAL TASK FORCE ON THE POLITICAL AND INTERNATIONAL IMPLICATIONS OF THE ENERGY CRISIS:

Energy: The Imperative for a Trilateral Approach

The Trilateral Task Force on the Political and International Implications of the Energy Crisis assumes that the era of cheap and plentiful oil is over. The industrial countries face major problems of adjustment to uncertain energy supplies, high costs, and new requirements in political relations. Some of these problems are immediate; some are for the coming decade of continuing dependence on Middle East oil; some involve planning for the longer run. They can be met successfully only with policies elaborated in concert rather than in competition. In *economics,* our countries must contend with the short and long term effects of shortages and price increases on their national economies and on the international trading and monetary system, and the need to make early decisions on the development of new sources of energy. In *politics,* the trend toward politicization of international economic relations will be strengthened by the situation of relative scarcity in energy. Policies aimed at inducing the producers to keep producing and exporting oil will be needed, as will efforts to avert calamity in countries unable to meet the high price of oil. Above all, the Trilateral countries must cope with mounting pressures at home and modify accepted habits and lifestyles, while avoiding destructive competition among themselves and preserving their democratic institutions.

Among the three Trilateral areas, Europe is threatened with economic and financial crisis at a time of political weakness and disunity. Japan is highly vulnerable because of its energy dependence. North America is in a comparatively strong position, but it cannot take refuge in a policy of self-sufficiency and display unconcern for Europe and Japan without provoking reactions adverse to all. Europe and Japan cannot expect U.S. and Canadian assistance unless they impose strict measures on themselves. Vigorous coordinated action can help them all to reduce their oil dependence on the Middle East in the next decade.

The imperative for cooperation suggests a common long-range strategy and the following specific recommendations: (1) *Conservation and efficiency of energy use* — Governments and private bodies should develop conservation programs on a priority basis, including investment, joint research, and generally agreed targets. (2) *Assuring safe and adequate supplies* — Trilateral countries should coordinate policies to maximize bargaining power with the oil-exporting states, while creating inducements for them to keep up supplies, and developing alternative sources. (3) *Emergency sharing* — They should agree now on a plan including (a) the definition of an emergency, (b) stockpiling, (c) conservation, (d) emergency production, and (e) allocation of supplies. (4) *Finance* — The consuming countries should aim to meet the impact of high oil prices by increasing exports to producers, recycling the latter group's balance-of-payments surplus funds to the countries which incurred the deficits, and providing help to those threatened with financial collapse. (5) *Sharing of technology and joint R & D* — Governments must promote an extensive sharing of technology designed to increase efficiency and develop new energy sources. Priorities in research have to be established on the main lines of effort in developing sources of energy for the post-oil age.

In their *relations with oil-producing countries,* the consuming countries must try to build a continuing relationship in which both sides have a stake. This collaboration should look ahead to the time when the oil age fades out. Bilateral deals or regional approaches should take place within an agreed strategy serving the interests of the Trilateral countries as a whole. On political matters, a greater accommodation of approaches to such questions as the Arab-Israeli conflict or arms sales to Persian Gulf states would contribute to harmonizing oil policy with political and military objectives. The Middle East states should be encouraged to view their oil policies in the broader context of security and cooperation. In *relations with the U.S.S.R. and China,* the Trilateral countries should explore the possibilities of obtaining increased energy supplies while avoiding any substantial dependence on these countries. The high costs and risks involved should be weighed against comparable investments elsewhere. In their *relations with the LDC's,* the developed countries should join in measures, to which the oil-producing countries should also contribute, to help the poorest nations threatened with disaster by price increases in oil and other essential products.

A master strategy is needed to set broad lines of policy for the Trilateral countries on the energy problem. An energy agency, logically one associated with the O.E.C.D., is required for consultation and coordination of policies.

The Trilateral Process

The report which follows is the joint responsibility of the three rapporteurs of the Trilateral Task Force on the Political and International Implications of the Energy Crisis, with Mr. John C. Campbell serving as principal drafter.

Although only the three rapporteurs are responsible for the analysis and conclusions, they were aided in their task by extensive trilateral consultations held during 1974 in Tokyo, Brussels and New York. The rapporteurs also took part in a conference on cooperation and development in the Mediterranean area held in Milan in which a number of prominent government officials, businessmen and academics from Europe and the Middle East took part. Among those consulted were:

Zbigniew Brzezinski, *Director, The Trilateral Commission*
George S. Franklin, *North American Secretary, The Trilateral Commission*
Wolfgang Hager, *European Secretary, The Trilateral Commission*
Rokuro Ishikawa, *Executive Vice President, Kajima Corporation*
Paul F. Langer, *Senior Social Scientist, The RAND Corporation*
Walter J. Levy, *President, W. J. Levy Consultants Corporation, Inc.*
Kiichi Miyazawa, *Member of the Diet (LDP); former Minister of International Trade and Industry*
Yoshihiko Morozumi, *Vice Chairman, Committee for Energy Policy and Promotion; former Vice Minister of International Trade and Industry*
Sohei Nakayama, *Counsellor, Industrial Bank of Japan*
M. V. Posner, *Director of Studies, Pembroke College, Cambridge University*
Ronald Ritchie, *Chairman, Institute for Research on Public Policy, Montreal*
Kiichi Saeki, *President, Nomura Research Institute of Technology and Economics*
Masao Sakisaka, *President, Institute of Energy Economics, Japan*
Dieter Schmitt, *Energy Institute of Cologne, University of Cologne*
Pierre Uri, *Atlantic Institute for International Affairs, Paris*
Carroll L. Wilson, *Professor of Management, Alfred P. Sloan School of Management, Massachusetts Institute of Technology*
Joseph A. Yager, *The Brookings Institution*

SCHEDULE OF TASK FORCE ACTIVITIES:

December 19, 1973 — Preliminary consultations in Washington involving Campbell, the Commission Director, the three Chairmen, the Secretaries, and members of The Brookings Institution.

March 15, 1974 — Meeting of North American Task Force in New York City.

March - April — Meetings of Japanese Task Force.

March 25-28 — Rapporteurs participate in tripartite energy meetings in Brussels sponsored by The Brookings Institution, the European Community Institute for University Studies, and the Japan Economic Research Center.

March 29 — Rapporteurs, Hager and Brzezinski meet in Brussels.

May 4-5 — Campbell, de Carmoy and Hager attend meeting of European and Arab businessmen, government officials and academics in Milan, sponsored by the European Community Commission and the Italian Institute of International Affairs.

May 6 — First draft of the report circulated.

May 7 — Meeting of Rapporteurs and Hager in Paris.

May 10 — Meeting of North American Task Force in New York City.

May 17 — Second draft of the report circulated.

May 30 — Second draft discussed at North American Commissioners meeting in New York City.

Early June — Third draft completed.

June 25 — Discussion of the report at the Executive Committee meeting in Brussels.

Energy: A Strategy for International Action

The international energy crisis presents a range of challenges to the Trilateral countries. Their response has been weak and inadequate, the task force concludes, and it recommends a broad program of action.

The report concentrates on three major problem areas, along with energy policy itself. One is relations with oil-exporters, especially those in the Middle East. How is the adjustment to be made between vital consumer interests and the exercise by the producers of their new "oil power"? Second are the strains induced and intensified among Trilateral countries themselves. The oil embargo and sharp rise in oil prices have tended so far to divide the three regions, and Western Europe within itself. Third are serious problems of internal adjustment and stress that lie ahead for the Trilateral countries in facing the societal implications of the crisis. These three sets of problems are interrelated. Trilateral solidarity, for instance, is affected by the approaches chosen to the oil-exporters and by the success of governments in handling domestic strains.

The task force recommends a broad, positive approach to the oil-exporters, without isolating the issue of price. The Trilateral countries should seek common and reciprocal interests with the exporters going far beyond oil, interests which can be furthered by cooperation in a variety of forms, bilateral and multilateral. It is suggested that the Trilateral Commission itself set up an expert group to seek unofficial discussions with OPEC representatives on a whole range of relevant issues. The oil issue in the Middle East cannot be separated from the Arab-Israeli conflict. The task force emphasizes the need for an early settlement and for an agreed North American-European-Japanese approach. In fact, Trilateral ideas on the general terms of a settlement are not widely different, based on the principle of non-acquisition of territory by force and the right of all states to secure existence.

While seeking positive relationships with the producers, the Trilateral countries must themselves cooperate to maintain their financial health in the face of existing oil prices and to establish arrangements for sharing energy in any future emergency resulting from cutoffs of Arab oil supplies. The task force applauds the emergency sharing plan proposed by the Energy Coordinating Group and recommends acceptance of this plan by all Trilateral countries.

For the medium term, through 1985, the Trilateral countries must start now to work toward reductions of their dependence on uncertain external energy sources. This requires action for both conservation and increased supplies. On conservation, the task force recommends that the annual rate of increase in energy consumption over the next decade be held below 2 percent in North America, 3 percent in Europe, and 4 percent in Japan. This is a substantial reduction from rates of increase prevailing before 1973. On increasing secure supplies, the task force sees the most immediate increases coming primarily from intensified production within the Trilateral community from known reserves of fossil fuels. The task force recommends that policy decisions on North Sea oil and gas development be taken on a European basis, and that Canada and the United States take Japanese and European needs into account in development of their own rich fossil fuel sources. If the solidarity and cooperation of the Trilateral countries is necessary and desirable for reducing dependence on OPEC, for emergency sharing, and for coping with high oil prices, then it should be valid as well for the development of known resources, whatever their location, within the Trilateral area.

For the much longer term, to the end of this century, the Trilateral countries should move now to outline cooperative energy research and development efforts, anticipating the end of the hydrocarbon age.

While not pessimistic about the long-term future, the task force sees a transitional period of extraordinary difficulty and adjustment ahead as Trilateral societies adapt to insecure, expensive, perhaps reduced energy supplies, and to slower economic growth. It is a real question whether the necessary sacrifices will in fact be accepted by powerful elements in the body politic. In such cases, there is instability whether a government tries to face the crisis or to avoid it. Countries must remain sensitive to each other's problems and agree on sharing burdens and shortages. The task force emphasizes the value of the O.E.C.D. and the International Energy Agency as structures for international cooperation.

The central thrust of this report is toward an agreed long-term energy strategy for the Trilateral countries. The specific recommendations are intended to give substance to that strategy and ensure its success.

The Trilateral Process

The report which follows is the joint responsibility of the three rapporteurs of the Trilateral Task Force on the Political and International Implications of the Energy Crisis, with Mr. John C. Campbell serving as principal drafter. The rapporteurs were aided in their task by extensive trilateral consultations. In each case, the consultants spoke for themselves as individuals and not as representatives of any institutions with which they are associated. Those consulted included the following:

Zbigniew Brzezinski, *Director, The Trilateral Commission*
Hélène Carrère d'Encausse, *Fondation Nationale des Sciences Politiques, Paris*
George S. Franklin, *North American Secretary, The Trilateral Commission*
Wolfgang Hager, *Research Institute of the German Society for Foreign Policy*
Rokuro Ishikawa, *Executive Vice President, Kajima Corporation*
Karl Kaiser, *Director of the Research Institute of the German Society for Foreign Policy*
Paul F. Langer, *Senior Social Scientist, The RAND Corporation*
Walter J. Levy, *President, W. J. Levy Consultants Corporation, Inc.*
Cesare Merlini, *Director of the Italian Institute for International Affairs*
Kiichi Miyazawa, *Member of the Diet (LDP); former Minister of International Trade and Industry*
Yoshihiko Morozumi, *Vice Chairman, Committee for Energy Policy and Promotion; former Vice Minister of International Trade and Industry*
Peter R. Odell, *Director of the Economics-Geography Institute, Erasmus University, Rotterdam*
Jean-Luc Pepin, P.C., *President, Interimco, Ltd., Ottawa*
Kiichi Saeki, *President, Nomura Research Institute of Technology and Economics*
Masao Sakisaka, *President, Japan Institute of Energy Economics*
Eric C. Sievwright, *President, E. C. Sievwright Associates, Ltd., Toronto*
Takao Tomitate, *Senior Economist, Japan Institute of Energy Economics*
Louis Turner, *Research Specialist, The Royal Institute of International Affairs, London*
Carroll L. Wilson, *Professor of Management, Alfred P. Sloan School of Management, Massachusetts Institute of Technology*
Joseph A. Yager, *The Brookings Institution*

SCHEDULE OF TASK FORCE ACTIVITIES:

June 25-26, 1974 — Executive Committee of Commission, meeting in Brussels, discusses earlier report of task force. Campbell and Kondo meet to consider outlines of current report.

October 1-2 — Rapporteurs and Brzezinski meet in Paris and consider first draft of report.

October 16 — Second draft of report completed and circulated among Commissioners and consultants.

October 22 — European consultants meet with de Carmoy in Bonn to consider second draft.

Late October — Campbell discusses second draft with North American consultants.

November — Kondo discusses second draft with Japanese task force.

November 25 — Third draft of report completed and circulated within Executive Committee of Commission.

December 9 — Discussion of the report at the Executive Committee meeting in Washington, D.C.

December 19 — Final draft of report completed for publication.

SUMMARY OF THE SECOND REPORT OF THE TASK FORCE
ON RELATIONS WITH DEVELOPING COUNTRIES:

OPEC, the Trilateral World, and the Developing Countries:
New Arrangements for Cooperation, 1976-1980

An extra $6 billion a year in Official Development Assistance (ODA) will be needed in the period 1976-80 to assure a 2% growth rate in per capita income in the approximately 30 low-income developing countries containing one billion of the world's people. Although there will be pressures to "write off" these countries if economic and political crises deepen in the Trilateral region, such a policy would be politically unrealistic as well as morally unacceptable. Moreover, a joint Trilateral-OPEC initiative that brings forth more capital for development would serve some very immediate Trilateral country interests. In a time of stagnant growth and rising unemployment, it is obviously advantageous to move funds from OPEC countries which cannot spend them on Trilateral country exports to developing countries who will.

Knowledgeable officials estimate that ODA from OPEC countries will reach approximately $3 billion a year in the 1976-80 period. In these same years, the Trilateral countries should, at a minimum, increase the size of their own ODA (about $9.4 billion in 1973 dollars) to keep pace with inflation. This will still leave $3 billion a year of ODA to be found.

To meet this need, it is proposed that a "Third Window" be opened in the World Bank to borrow $3 billion a year of OPEC country funds at 8% and lend it to low-income countries at 3%, in loans with 20-year maturities and 4-year grace periods, in each of the years 1976-80. This would require an annual interest subsidy of $900 million, of which $100 million could be raised from World Bank earnings, $500 million from Trilateral countries, and $300 million from OPEC countries.

The "Third Window" fund should be managed by a tripartite governing body, with representation and voting power equally shared between Trilateral countries, OPEC countries, and other developing countries. Moreover, to encourage the participation of the OPEC countries in the regular activities of the Bank and Fund, OPEC quotas and voting rights should be raised from the present 5% to between 15 and 20%.

The Trilateral Process

The report which follows is the joint responsibility of the three rapporteurs of the Trilateral Task Force on Relations with Developing Countries, with Professor Richard N. Gardner serving as principal drafter.

Although only the three rapporteurs are responsible for the analysis and conclusions, they were aided in their task by extensive consultations with experts from the trilateral regions, the developing countries, and various international organizations. In each case, the consultants spoke for themselves as individuals and not as the representatives of any institutions to which they belong. Those consulted included the following:

Michel van den Abeele, *Chef de Cabinet of Henri Simonet, Vice-President of the Commission of the European Communities*

C. Fred Bergsten, *Senior Fellow, The Brookings Institution*

Zbigniew Brzezinski, *Director, The Trilateral Commission*

Jacques Alain le Chartier de Sedouy, *Chef de Cabinet of Claude Cheysson, Member of the Commission of the European Communities*

Claude Cheysson, *Member of the Commission of the European Communities*

Richard N. Cooper, *Professor of Economics, Yale University*

Gamani Corea, *Secretary-General of UNCTAD*

William B. Dale, *Deputy Managing Director, International Monetary Fund*

Count Etienne Davignon, *Director of Political Affairs, Belgian Foreign Ministry*

Guy Erb, *Overseas Development Council*

Clyde Farnsworth, *European Economic Correspondent, The New York Times*

George S. Franklin, *North American Secretary, The Trilateral Commission*

James Grant, *President, Overseas Development Council*

Joseph Greenwald, *United States Ambassador to the European Community*

Ravi Gulhati, *Director, Development Economics Department, International Bank for Reconstruction and Development*

Nurul Islam, *Deputy Chairman of Planning Commission, Government of Bangladesh*

Attila Karaosmanoglu, *Chief Economist, Europe, Middle East, and North Africa Regional Office, International Bank for Reconstruction and Development*

Abderahman Khene, *Secretary-General of OPEC*

Israel Klabin, *Klabin Irmaos & Cia., Rio de Janeiro*

Emile van Lennep, *Director-General of OECD*

Joseph Luns, *Secretary-General of NATO*

Robert S. McNamara, *President, International Bank for Reconstruction and Development*

208

Benedict Meynell, *Director, External Relations Division, Commission of the European Communities*

Cecilio J. Morales, *Manager, Economic and Social Development Department, Inter-American Development Bank*

Enrique Perez-Cisneros, *Special Representative, Europe, Inter-American Development Bank*

J. J. Polak, *Director of Research Department, International Monetary Fund*

Raúl Prebisch, *Special Representative of the Secretary-General for the United Nations Emergency Operation, United Nations*

Gustav Ranis, *Director, Economic Growth Center, Yale University*

Mohamed Shoaib, *Vice-President, International Bank for Reconstruction and Development*

A. Maxwell Stamp, *economic consultant, London*

Ernest Stern, *Director, Development Policy, International Bank for Reconstruction and Development*

Ernest Sturc, *Director, Exchange and Trade Relations, International Monetary Fund*

Anthony F. Tuke, *Chairman, Barclays Bank International, Ltd.*

Kaye Whiteman, *Information Office, Development Cooperation Directory, European Commission*

Maurice Williams, *Chairman, Development Assistance Committee, OECD*

SCHEDULE OF TASK FORCE ACTIVITIES:

June 25, 1974 — Executive Committee of Commission, meeting in Brussels, discusses earlier report of task force.

September 29 — Gardner and Okita consult with thirteen experts in Washington, D.C.

September 30 - October 3 — Gardner and Okita continue consultations in Washington, D.C., during Annual Meetings of World Bank and International Monetary Fund.

Early November — Gardner and Udink carry on extensive consultations in Europe.

Late November — First draft of report completed and circulated within Executive Committee of Commission.

December 9 — Discussion of the report at the Executive Committee meeting in Washington, D.C.

Mid-December — First draft circulated to all Commission members.

January - February, 1975 — Gardner continues consultations on first draft.

February 28 — Final draft of report completed for publication.